Authentic Evangelism

Other Books by William Powell Tuck

The Bible as Our Guide for Spiritual Growth (editor)

Facing Grief and Death

Getting Past the Pain: Making Sense of Life's Darkness

A Glorious Vision: The Worship Symbols in the Sanctuary of the St. Matthews Baptist Church, Louisville, Kentucky

Knowing God: Religious Knowledge in the Theology of John Baillie

The Lord's Prayer Today

Ministry: An Ecumenical Challenge (editor)

Our Baptist Tradition

The Struggle for Meaning (editor)

The Way for All Seasons

Authentic Evangelism

Sharing the Good News with Sense and Sensitivity

WILLIAM POWELL TUCK

Judson Press
Valley Forge

Authentic Evangelism
Sharing the Good News with Sense and Sensitivity

© 2002 by Judson Press, Valley Forge, PA 19482-0851

Unless otherwise indicated, Scripture is taken from the Revised Standard Version of the Bible, copyright 1946, 1952, 1971 by the Division of Christian Education of the National Council of the Churches of Christ in the USA. Used by permission.
Other Scriptures quotations are marked as follows:
The Contemporary English Version, © 1991, 1995 American Bible Society. Used by permission. (CEV)
The Holy Bible, King James Version. (KJV)
HOLY BIBLE: NEW INTERNATIONAL VERSION, copyright © 1973, 1978, 1984 by International Bible Society. Used by permission of Zondervan Bible Publishers. All rights reserved. (NIV)
The New Revised Standard Version of the Bible, copyright © 1989 by the Division of Christian Education of the National Council of the Churches of Christ in the United States of America. Used by permission. All rights reserved. (NRSV)

Library of Congress Cataloging-in-Publication Data

Tuck, William Powell, 1934–
    Authentic evangelism : sharing the Good News with sense and sensitivity / William Powell Tuck.
        p. cm.
    Includes bibliographical references.
    ISBN 0-8170-1415-2 (pbk. : alk. paper)
    1. Evangelistic work. I. Title.
    BV3790 .T76   2002
    269'.2—dc21   2001050506

Printed in the U.S.A.

08 07 06 05 04 03 02
10 9 8 7 6 5 4 3 2 1

To my mother church,
West Lynchburg Baptist,
where I first learned to share the gospel

CONTENTS

FOREWORD

*A*UTHENTIC EVANGELISM BY WILLIAM POWELL TUCK IS A substantive contribution to the church's literature on evangelism. Tuck helps his readers recover the biblical beauty and the theological fragrance of evangelism. This is a book that will appeal to those who have been turned off by the ugliness and stench of shallow, modern imitations of real evangelism.

It is evident that the author has drunk deeply from the fountains of the Bible, pastoral experience, and books on evangelism. These pages are laced with the tapestry of solid scriptural interpretation, striking illustrations, and apt quotations from other sources.

I was impressed by Tuck's style of writing as well as by his substantive content. His chapters have structure, but the skeleton is never obtrusive and not too evident. His readers will not be confronted with so many bones that they will cry out, "Where's the beef?"

Tuck does not use worn-out phases, technical theological jargon, or words unknown to ordinary churchgoers. Nor does he turn up the volume of his rhetoric in order to make evangelists out of reluctant witnesses. Instead, he reasons with, woos, and confronts his readers as a fellow pilgrim who is still pressing forward in the Abrahamic journey of faith.

This book represents pastoral evangelism at its best— evangelism that is both sensible and sensitive. Pastors can learn from it how to challenge their parishioners to share their faith with non-Christians. Christians who want to share their faith with lost loved ones, friends, neighbors, and acquaintances can learn from it how to share their faith without being offensive.

We need more books on evangelism from seasoned, practicing pastors. Note how few of the volumes in Tuck's selected bibliography are by authors who were actually shepherding congregations when they wrote about evangelism. I see *Authentic Evangelism* by Bill Tuck in the same tradition as David H. C. Read's *Go Make Disciples* and David Watson's *I Believe in Evangelism.*

Delos Miles
Professor Emeritus of Evangelism
Campbell University Divinity School
Buies Creek, North Carolina

PREFACE

*I*F YOU ARE A CHRISTIAN TODAY, YOU MADE THAT RELIGIOUS commitment because someone at some place and time in your life shared the good news of Jesus Christ with you. You had to hear before you could respond. The growth of the Christian church through the centuries has been carried forward in that same way—one person telling another or several others about God's redeeming grace through his Son, Jesus Christ. If Christians tried to keep the gospel a secret and refused to tell others the good news they have heard, the church would soon die. Evangelism—the sharing of God's good news between two or more individuals—is an indispensable part of the heartbeat of the church. In a vital church, evangelism will pulsate with conviction and power.

Jesus Christ left an unmistakable imperative for his followers: "Go therefore and make disciples of all nations" (Matthew 28:19). He told his first disciples, "Follow me and I will make you fishers of men" (Mark 1:17). Our Lord acknowledged that the need was great and more evangelists were essential to accomplish his mission. "The harvest is plentiful, but the laborers are few; pray therefore the Lord of the harvest to send out laborers into his harvest" (Luke 10:2). "You shall be my witnesses" (Acts 1:8). This was the charge our risen Lord gave to his disciples. The mandate of our Lord is clear—his disciples have been commissioned to be evangelists. But even when we affirm that mandate from our Lord, many of us are not clear how to do the work of an evangelist or we are turned off by the fanatical or arrogant personalities of some professional or lay evangelists. It is unfortunate that many have let distorted or objectionable persons or methods keep them from doing what our Lord has challenged his disciples to do.

Our challenge is to present authentic evangelism—that is, evangelism distinguished from the false, distorted, or pseudo versions that turn many people off. Authentic evangelism is patterned after the methods of the Master and his disciples. Authentic evangelism is a way of sharing the Good News that demonstrates respect and concern for the total person with whom the message is communicated. It does not want to manipulate, coerce, or frighten another person, but rather seeks to expose an individual to the love, grace, forgiveness, and acceptance of our Lord. As we seek to share the Good News with another person, we draw upon the best resources we have today to present the gospel message and we strive to do so in a way that is appealing and not offensive.

The New Testament Greek word for evangelism has a beautiful root. The English noun *evangelism* contains the word *angel*. An angel is a messenger who brings good news about God, and that is what an evangelist is: a person who brings to another the good news about God's revelation and redemption through Jesus Christ.

This volume is sent forth with the hope that more Christians will be inspired to share the wonderful story of God's love. I pray that we will be able to say with the apostle Paul, "I am not ashamed of the gospel" (Romans 1:16).

Some Thoughts on How to Use This Book

1. A Sunday school class might use this book as a study guide in evangelism for a period of ten weeks. The questions at the end of each chapter might be assigned to various class members to provide discussion.

2. The deacons, evangelism committee, or a selected group of church leaders might use this book as a resource for motivation and planning for evangelistic efforts in the local congregation.

3. A group of pastors in a community or association might study and discuss this book to stimulate preaching and teaching on the theme of evangelism.

4. This book could provide a pastor or a selected lay leader a resource for teaching or preaching on evangelism at Sunday or midweek services or on other occasions.

5. Youth leaders or parachurch group leaders might use this book as a resource to equip youth or others in evangelism. The sessions could include hands-on training.

6. This book could be a source of discussion for a lay or ministerial book club.

ACKNOWLEDGMENTS

I WANT TO EXPRESS MY APPRECIATION TO CAROLYN STICE, MY secretary of ten years, who willingly typed this manuscript through several editions; to Ida Helm, who diligently proofed these pages and offered her suggestions; and to Helen Crenshaw, who helped me get the manuscript into its final shape.

CHAPTER 1

The *Call*
TO
EVANGELISM

SEVERAL YEARS AGO I SAT IN MY STUDY ON A BREATHTAKINGLY beautiful autumn afternoon looking out the window at the multicolored leaves that covered the landscape. The red, orange, and yellow leaves seemed to radiate in the bright sunlight. I turned back to my reading but was interrupted by a gentle knock on my study door.

I opened the door and found a young college student standing there. She smiled slightly at me and asked if she might have a few minutes to talk with me. I invited her in, and she sat down in a chair near my desk and explained that she had been coming to our church for several weeks. She said that going to church was a new experience for her, since her family had never been involved in church. Several of her friends had encouraged her to come with them to our worship service, and she had.

"I would like to know more about this Jesus Christ of whom you have spoken," she said. "I don't know if I understand, nor am I ready or willing to begin making that kind of commitment. But I would like to know more about what it means to be a Christian. Is there anything you can say or give me that would help me?"

Here was a young woman who was unfamiliar with the Christian faith yet hungered to know more about what it meant to be a Christian. We talked for some time, and I tried to share with her the gospel in a "nutshell." I listened and responded to questions from this seeker who did not want cliches or easy answers. She wanted a faith that was real and meaningful. I shared with her a little booklet by Leslie Weatherhead entitled *The Presence of Jesus* and asked her to read it and then come back to see me so that I could hear her reaction to it and respond to any questions she might have.

Several weeks later this young woman came back to see me. We talked about the booklet, and I responded to her questions about religion. Her bright mind would not settle for a simplified solution to the tough problems of life or to a three-step or parrot-like repeated plan of salvation. She asked hard questions, and I tried to give honest answers. After we had talked for some time, she said she wanted to surrender her life to Christ. "My experience may not be the doorway through which many have come to know Christ as Savior," she said, "but this is my experience, and it is real to me. I believe God loves me and will accept me as I am as I commit myself in faith to Jesus Christ."

Few persons with whom I have talked have wrestled with as many tough questions and hard issues of the faith as this young woman did. She had learned not to discredit her own experience because it was not like that of others. I have discovered that God never has just one path into the human soul. God has as many variations as there are people. God works in God's own way in reaching into the hearts and minds of people.

Some may try to push another into making a commitment to Christ. Some well-meaning evangelist, professional or lay, may assault another with his or her approach to religion. Sometimes in a pushy, offensive, arrogant way, an evangelist demands what another must believe and what pathway that person must take to become a Christian. Many people are turned off by this approach. Others identify evangelism with revivalism or emotionalism. Still others identify evangelism with a white-suited evangelist who yells at the top of his voice.

Sadly, the good word *evangelism* has been corrupted. This beautiful word has been twisted and distorted into something distasteful. Nevertheless, evangelism is an authentic ministry of the church, and there has never been a time when the need for evangelism was more apparent. Voices cry out from all around us for direction, meaning, and purpose in life, and the good news of Jesus Christ offers wholeness and redemption. But we have to learn the best way, medium, style, and approach to share the Good News for the age in which we are living. Our challenge is no easy task.

The Drift Away from Evangelism

Many contemporary churches have shifted away from the early church's commitment to evangelism. What has caused this to happen? Many reasons could be listed. Here I suggest just a few.

A Naive Assumption

The first reason I would suggest for the church's shift away from a commitment to evangelism is that many people in our churches have a naive assumption that everybody in American society is already a Christian. Although most church historians describe our country as post-Christian and multireligious, many people still call the United States a Christian country. Many think that being a Christian is like being an American. If you are born in this country, you are an American, and that makes you a Christian. This false conclusion has led many to feel that there is no need to bother others by trying to share their faith with them. But this civil religion is a far cry from authentic New Testament Christianity.

Look around you and you will notice quickly that few people have any real sense of sin today. Many people attach no meaning to the word *sin* and seldom worry about what they have done that is wrong unless they get caught.

You may have heard the story about a young preacher who went with an older evangelist to visit some homes in a neighborhood near their church. As they approached the door of a spacious mansion, they saw two Cadillacs and a Mercedes in the driveway and a large boat parked in the side yard. Looking through the glass door, the two men noticed a man sitting in front of a gigantic television set. The man was wearing Bermuda shorts and sipping a can of beer. The young man said to his older friend, "What good news do we have to tell this man?"

Do you hear the message from this young man's lips? He assumed that as long as people are wealthy and successful they have no spiritual needs. This would imply that they have no need of God or Christ. They have money! Often we are unaware of people's deeper needs for meaning, purpose, understanding, forgiveness, hope, and love. Sometimes they are lonely, frustrated, depressed, and confused, and they long for wholeness and faith. We have a word of hope they need to hear.

Distorted Image

Second, *evangelism* has become a negative word today because of the distorted images we often see in society. Who among us has not been the victim of some preacher who has tried to browbeat us, twist our arms, and make us feel guilty? I have sat in services where preachers have looked at little six-year-old children and said, "If you don't come to Jesus today, you will burn in hell forever." I have seen evangelists use different color cards as they talked with preschoolers. They would tell the children that the black card represented the children's sin, the red card the blood of Jesus, and the white card the change Jesus would make in their lives. Then these evangelists would tell the preschoolers, "If you don't come to Jesus today, you are doomed forever!"

I have walked down the streets of New Orleans and have been accosted by street preachers who described the awfulness of hell as though they had been on a recent tour. I once saw a car in Texas with Scripture quotations painted all over it. Loudspeakers from the car blurted out, "Come to Jesus and be saved." These attempts at evangelism are repulsive to most people who are exposed to them.

Tragically, the corruption of something good has caused many to reject evangelism. Recently my wife was reading a book dealing with the faith of some of our country's founding fathers. She came across a line from Thomas Jefferson, who had been reading a lengthy work by Joseph Priestley dealing with corruption in religion. Jefferson said, "I thought I had rejected Christianity, but I had rejected only a corruption of Christianity."[1] Don't reject evangelism. Reject the corruption of evangelism.

Ignorant of the Faith

Third, evangelism has also waned in our day because many Christians are ignorant of the real content of the Christian faith they claim. Many church members do not understand the basic message of Christianity, nor are they able to explain the cardinal words of their religion, such as *faith, sin, salvation, grace,* or *the providence of God.* They cling to fuzzy notions of Christianity and have never ventured into a pilgrimage to grow into a more mature faith. They remain like small children and stand on the edge of their religion, never growing into a deep understanding of the teachings of Christ and the Bible. When they are challenged to explain some aspects of their belief, they are often unable to expound the simplest basic facts of Christianity. It is almost impossible for these persons to be evangelists.

No Clear Understanding of Evangelism

Fourth, evangelism has fallen on hard times because of the claims by some that everything the church does in ministry is evangelistic. That assertion often is actually an excuse that keeps a church from being evangelistic. Yes, everything we do as a church should point persons to the ultimate source of why we do ministry. Whether it is youth work, nursing home visitation, support groups, or counseling, the love of Christ should motivate us. But most of these ministries are not evangelism per se. They point to Christ and prepare persons to hear the Good News, but the Good News has to be shared at some point.

Timidity

Fifth, evangelism is hindered because some Christians are too embarrassed and timid to share their faith. For some reason, shyness overtakes persons when they have a chance to share their faith. I understand these feelings. I can remember several occasions when I was a young minister and went to call at a certain home that I would pause and pray silently before I knocked on the door, "Oh, Lord, don't let them be at home." Many are timid because they do not know how to approach another person with the Good News. Training and experience can help us overcome these feelings of inadequacy and fear of failure. Some Christians are embarrassed because they do not want to appear as fanatics. If we share our faith naturally and without pressure, we will not have to worry about this kind of label.

Narrow-Mindedness

Sixth, sometimes a strong hindrance to persons sharing their faith is the fear of being accused of narrow-mindedness. In our society today many people do not want to be seen as putting down another person's religion by asserting one's own understanding of God. Today so much emphasis is placed on tolerance that some feel that it is unpopular or antisocial to share their Christian faith with another. Thus, many choose to be mute rather than risk offending someone by talking about the Christian gospel.

Let's be honest and affirm that we want to respect another person's religious perspective, whether it is Hinduism, Buddhism, Islam, Judaism, materialism, or atheism. Some assert that all religious paths lead to God, so why try to "push" the Christian faith? If a person has another religious background, such as Hinduism, for example, you might study that religion and be informed. Affirm the good tenets in that religion and then encourage your friend to see the added dimension that Christ offers to understanding God and life. Point out in the Book of Acts, for example, how the apostle Paul helped his fellow Jews to see how Jesus fulfilled the Jewish hope of the promised Messiah by citing their own Scriptures (Acts13:13–43). Note also how Paul challenged the Athenians to see that the "unknown god" they worshiped was the Christ he proclaimed to them (Acts 17:16–34). Philip (Acts 8:26–40), Peter (Acts 9:32–43; 10:1–48), Paul, Silas, and others (Acts 17ff.) drew upon the religious traditions they encountered but freely shared the message about Christ who had changed their lives. Paul, Peter, and other believers of Jesus noted the lessons they had learned from Judaism or other religions but added their affirmation of how Christ fulfilled or completed God's revelation to humanity.

By being tolerant and respectful of another person's belief, you may find that person more open and willing to listen to your message. The gospel story shared gently and naturally may find a willing ear. You at least can share your Christian tradition without finding it so difficult.

One of my former church members told me how he was in a foreign country on business and was invited to the home of one of his business associates who was a Hindu. While there the conversation turned to his religious faith. He shared his beliefs naturally with them without condemning their beliefs and by affirming the good points in their religion. By taking this approach, he found a family who wanted to know more about the Christian faith. I helped him get some copies of the New Testament in their own language and some booklets that described Christian beliefs. This young man spoke to me about his sense of excitement of going back to that country and dialoguing with that family about religion and hopefully leading them to Christ.

If you are respectful and tolerant of another person's religion, you need not find it difficult to speak openly to that person about what you believe. As Christians we believe that God has shared the divine Presence uniquely with humanity through Christ, but to communicate this message to others, we have to gain their respect, acceptance, and willingness to hear.

A Loss of Mission

Seventh, another reason evangelism has suffered is that many churches have lost their sense of mission. Apathy has overtaken church members, and few seem concerned with sharing the message of salvation. They feel no sense of compulsion to share the good news of God's grace, so they sit back and wait for somebody else to carry the message.

Several years ago I heard a parable that I have not forgotten. On one of the coasts of our country, there were some lifeguards who courageously launched their boats out into rough seas to rescue persons who were drowning. One day the lifeguards rescued a drowning man, and he was so grateful that he gave them enough money to build a lovely lifeguard house on the beach. It was a first-class place. The house was carpeted, air-conditioned, and nicely furnished. Beds were provided so the lifeguards could rest. Soon the lifeguards began to spend most of their time inside their house. There were cries for help in the waters, but the lifeguards were so busy enjoying their house they did not hear them. Soon the lifeguards became more and more comfortable in their house and could not hear the cries for help from drowning men and women at all.

The church, if it is the church, cannot be content with remaining in its buildings. We are called to go out into the highways and the hedges to share the good news of Jesus Christ with all people. The heart of every Christian needs to beat with a sense of urgency to share the love of God with others. Since many of those who need to hear the gospel may never come into our church buildings, we have to go into the world and tell them about God's redemption. The church cannot—must not—be preoccupied with itself and forget those outside its walls who need to hear the message of salvation.

Without evangelism the church will die. The church is always one generation away from extinction. If the church is not careful, we may let everything else we do, as important as all our other ministries are, keep us from doing the work of an evangelist. Genuine evangelism is not concerned primarily with numbers, results, or methods. True evangelism seeks to lead people to Christ and to become his disciples. Genuine evangelism is interested more in making disciples than converts. Those who are genuinely won to Christ will want to grow in their knowledge of him and mature in their faith. They will not be content with merely "meeting" Christ.

• • •

Don't let the distortions of evangelism keep you from being authentically evangelistic. If we reject evangelism, we lose the central message of the gospel itself. The writer of the Gospel of John reminds his readers that the reason he wrote it was "that you may believe that Jesus is the Christ, the Son of God, and that believing you may have life in his name" (John 20:31). From the beginning, the church was evangelistic, and it continues its existence through evangelism. Theologian Emil Brunner has reminded us that "the church exists by mission as fire exists by burning."[2]

The Call to Evangelize

You and I, as members of the church of Christ, should respond positively to the call to be evangelists for many reasons, a few of which I discuss here.

Share in Obedience to the Command of God

First, we should respond to God's call to be evangelists because it is God's command. In Genesis we read that God commanded Abraham to leave his country and go in search of a new land that God would give him. God promised that Abraham would be a blessing to all nations. When Israel turned inward and became consumed with their own nationalism, they corrupted the call of Abraham. God had called them out as a nation not merely to bless them, but that God might work through them to bless all nations.

Jesus called his disciples to be fishers of people. He summoned Peter and Andrew with the words, "Come with me! I will teach you how to bring in people instead of fish" (Mark 1:17, CEV). Jesus commanded his followers, in the Great Commission, "Go therefore and make disciples of all nations" (Matthew 28:19–20). And in Acts 1:8 he said, "You shall be my witnesses . . . to the end of the earth." You may have seen people wearing a small fishhook on their lapel or dress to symbolize that they are Christians. I think a better symbol would be a net. As we witness for Christ, we do not want to hurt people but help them. A net catches more, and it is truer symbolically to the biblical understanding of what it is to be fishers of men and women in the name of Christ. Our call to evangelize begins with Christ's command to go and make disciples.

Share Out of Our Christian Responsibility

Second, we notice in the New Testament from the example of the early Christians that evangelism was the responsibility of every Christian. Evangelism was not left to a few preachers; every single Christian became an evangelist. After Andrew was convinced that Jesus was the Messiah, the first thing he did was to tell his brother, Simon, about Jesus (John 1:41). Philip in turn shared his encounter with Jesus with Nathanael (John 1:45). Following her conversation with Jesus at the well, the Samaritan woman immediately told others in her village to "come, see," and they came and "many more believed" (John 4:29,41). A leper was cleansed by Jesus, and he "began to talk freely" (Mark 1:45). The apostle Paul shared his conversion experience with others in Jerusalem (Acts 22:1–21) and before King Agrippa (Acts 26:1–28). The first thing Mary Magdalene did after meeting the risen Lord was to tell the disciples, "I have seen the Lord" (John 20:18).

When a person was converted, that individual began to share the good news of Christ with others. He or she didn't say, "Now wait a minute—I have to go see if I can find Simon Peter or the local pastor and let the 'expert' tell someone about Christ." Every Christian was an evangelist.

Elton Trueblood has reminded us that "in the beginning of the Christian cause all were ministers. *Member* equaled *evangelist* equaled *missionary.* There was no place within the society for the observer, the mere supporter or the nominal member."[3] All Christians were and should be evangelists. One of the great tragedies of the church is that its members have left evangelism to the clergy. If evangelism is left to the clergy alone, the church will quickly die. Laypersons can often be far better evangelists than clergy, because they are with other persons at work, in leisure, and a thousand other places. Thus, they have more occasions and opportunities to witness for Christ.

Share Out of Our Concern for Others

Third, we should be evangelists not only because of the command of Christ and the example of the early church, but out of our own concern for other people. Are you really concerned for others around you who do not have a saving knowledge of Jesus Christ? Are you genuinely concerned that your coworkers, neighbors, and friends do not know the good news of God's love? Does it make you sad? Do you not have a Christian duty to share the knowledge of God's love with them? Out of concern for other people, will you not want to share the good news of Jesus Christ with them? We are called not only to be disciples (learners) but apostles (those sent). When we really care, we will share.

Share Out of the Love We Experience in Christ

Fourth, we will want to be evangelists because we will speak out of the love that we have experienced in Christ. Paul says, "For Christ's love compels us" (2 Corinthians 5:14, NIV). The love of Christ! Because you and I have experienced the love of God in Jesus Christ, have known his forgiving grace, and have found direction, purpose, goals, and meaning for our lives, we will feel compelled to share that love with others. How can we keep it to ourselves? The basic motive for evangelism arises out of God's love for us and the love we now feel for God. If we have really experienced the power of the grace of Christ, how can we not share it?

Suppose you had a secret cure for cancer and walked through a cancer ward in a hospital. As you walked by the patients, you fluffed up their pillows and said, "I hope you are feeling better today." You were cordial, but you never shared the secret of the cure with them. Ridiculous! Just as the love of Christ would compel you to share the cure with those who were dying, the same love compels you to share Christ's gospel of life with those who are spiritually dead.

Share Out of Joy

You will also want to share the good news of Christ with others out of the joy you have experienced in God's love. If you really know God's grace, your gratitude will motivate you to speak about the inner joy you have. A professional baseball player was once asked, "Are the legs the first thing to go in baseball?" "No, it's not the legs," he responded, "but the inner desire." When you have no sense of gratitude for God's love, you will feel no inner compulsion to tell others about Christ. But when you have experienced this inner joy and have felt the redeeming grace of God, like C. S. Lewis, you will be surprised by joy and will desire to pass it on. I think we all need to discover what Harry Emerson Fosdick has called "the fine art of making goodness attractive."[4] When the joy of Christ beats in our heart, we will radiate a light that will enable us to be "letters of recommendation . . . known and read by all" (2 Corinthians 3:2).

Composer Joseph Haydn was asked one day why his music was always so animated and cheerful. He replied, "I cannot make it otherwise. I write according to the thoughts I feel; when I think of God, my heart is so full of joy that the notes leap and dance as they leave my pen; and since God has given me a cheerful heart . . . I serve him with a cheerful spirit."[5] Today we sing the hymn "I Love to Tell the Story" with great enthusiasm. I hope that you really do love to tell the gospel story and that you will indeed tell it to others.

• • •

An ancient legend says that when Jesus returned to heaven the angel Gabriel asked him about his plans for continuing his work on earth. Jesus said, "I have chosen twelve ordinary men to be my disciples." The archangel asked, "But what if they fail?" Jesus replied, "I have no other plan." We are his disciples—learners—but let us remember that we are also apostles—those who have been sent to share the marvelous good news of Christ with all people. We must not fail!

Notes

1. Edwin S. Gaustad, *Faith of Our Fathers* (San Francisco: Harper & Row, 1987), 98.

2. Emil Brunner, *The Word and the World* (London: SCM Press, 1931), 108.

3. Elton Trueblood, *Alternative to Futility* (New York: Harper & Brothers, 1948), 73.

4. Harry Emerson Fosdick, *The Hope of the World* (New York: Harper & Brothers, 1933), 195.

5. Karl Geiringer, *Haydn: A Creative Life in Music* (New York: W. W. Norton & Co., 1946), 133.

Questions for Thought and Discussion

1. Do you agree with the writer that evangelism has been corrupted and that many persons are turned off by it today? Give reasons or examples in support of or against this conclusion.

2. What do you believe is the main reason the contemporary church has drifted away from evangelism? Why do you think this is so?

3. Can the church genuinely claim that everything it does is evangelistic and that its members never have to share a spoken word to anyone about the faith? What will happen to the church if this approach is taken?

4. Discuss times that you have been reluctant to share the faith with others because you felt inadequate, timid, embarrassed, or poorly equipped. Let each person in your group take a few moments to speak to this issue; then ask for suggestions for ways to overcome this reluctance.

5. Define the meaning of the word *evangelism*. What is the relationship of evangelism to the good news that Jesus came to proclaim?

6. Give at least five reasons why every Christian should be willing to be an evangelist for Christ. Can anyone excuse himself or herself from sharing the faith with others? Why is evangelism not primarily the work of the pastor, but of the laypersons in a church?

7. How do you react to the writer's suggestion that not to share the gospel with another is like having a cure for cancer and not sharing that cure with dying people? Is it really that urgent and essential that each of us be willing to witness to others? Why or why not?

CHAPTER 2

Jesus:
Our *Model*
FOR
EVANGELISM

A MAN AND HIS PASTOR WERE ENGAGED IN CONVERSATION about evangelism. "I really do not believe in evangelism," the man said. "I don't understand that," replied the pastor. "It is a New Testament teaching." "Well, I know," said the man. "It may be a New Testament teaching, but I only believe in following the teachings of Jesus."

How confused that man was! Evangelism certainly originated with our Lord himself. In fact, Jesus modeled authentic evangelism for us.

Although theologians and New Testament scholars have written thick books in which they have tried to explain the meaning of the word *gospel,* Mark summarized in two verses the gospel that Jesus preached (Mark 1:14–15). He wrote that Jesus came into Galilee preaching the good news of God. Jesus said that the time was fulfilled, and the kingdom of God was now present. Then he commanded his hearers to repent and believe the good news.

Jesus came announcing that the time for God's reign was imminent. The Roman roadways and culture, the universal

Greek language and philosophy, and the dispersal of the Jews around the world made the time ripe for God's Son to come. Paul expressed it this way: "When the time had fully come, God sent forth his Son" (Galatians 4:4). The kingdom of God—God's reign, rule, and sovereignty—was about to be instituted by Jesus.

Following his announcement that the new order was at hand, Jesus issued an appeal: Repent. Jesus did not hesitate to call persons to repentance. He called them to change their minds, to turn around and go in a new direction. "Look, the new order is present. Believe the good news. Believe, commit yourself to the way of God, and follow that truth." He called his hearers to respond to the proclamation of the good news that the new order had broken into time.

Television and radio reports of hurricane Fran captivated many people several years ago. Suppose you and I lived on the seacoast and heard that a hurricane like Fran was approaching with winds of 170 miles per hour. As the hurricane approached, television and radio announcers declared: "It is time to evacuate the area. Follow Main Street out of town and proceed north until you reach the designated safe areas." Most of those who heard the announcement would follow the advice, yet some would choose not to go. Others might be engaged in work or recreation and not hear the message. The announcement was made nevertheless. Yet only those who heard and understood would respond and be safe.

Jesus announced the good news that God's kingdom was breaking into history. He called on people to believe, respond, and repent, but only those who took him at his word and responded would follow him and be delivered.

Jesus' Concern for Persons

As Jesus, the master teacher, went throughout Galilee preaching the good news about God's kingdom, he demonstrated through his words and life the model for evangelism.

The basic principle he taught was his concern for people. You can always tell what is important to a person by what that person gives priority to in life—job, country, institution, family, wealth, fame, recreation, and so on. The Gospels reveal that Jesus' first priority was people. He took time to talk with people he met along the roadside, by a well, in the synagogues, in a friend's home. People were constantly interrupting him, and he paused to listen and talk with them. Wherever Jesus traveled he responded to the people who reached out to him.

One day in a mob of people, a woman with an issue of blood reached out and touched the edge of his garment. Jesus asked, "Who touched me?" (Luke 8:45, NIV). Power went out of him, and he responded to an individual in need. The personal concern of Jesus is seen as he reached out to blind Bartimaeus and when he noticed the poor widow in the temple, the crippled man by the pool of Siloam, and dozens of others who crossed his path daily. The Gospel writers refer to at least thirty-five personal contacts Jesus had with persons face to face. Jesus' personal concern was evidenced when he declared: "What man of you, if he has one sheep and it falls into a pit on the sabbath, will not lay hold of it and lift it out? Of how much more value is a man than a sheep?" (Matthew 12:11–12). "People were not made for the good of the Sabbath. The Sabbath was made for the good of people" (Mark 2:27, CEV).

To Jesus, people were more important than institutions, public meetings, personal success, traditions, laws, or anything else. His priority was with people. "Are not two sparrows sold for a penny? And not one of them will fall to the ground without your Father's will. . . . Fear not, therefore; you are of more value than many sparrows" (Matthew 10:29–31). Birds are valued by God, but people are much more important than birds.

The Gospels record that Jesus showed his concern for people by associating with men and women from every walk of life. He did not hesitate to associate with people who were classified as sinners and outcasts. He even ate meals in the homes of some tax collectors who were ostracized by other Jews. Jesus talked with women who had bad reputations. He reached out and touched lepers who were untouchables. He often showed concern for the poor and needy. But Jesus reached out to the wealthy as well. He ate meals in the homes of Levi and Zacchaeus. He also had time for children, women, the young and old, the confused, those who were searching, and those needing help. Jesus made time for people everywhere. The Gospels record at least three episodes in which he ate meals in the homes of Pharisees. Jesus associated with all kinds of people.

Those Who Are "Lost"

The most common word Jesus used to describe those who had not responded to the gospel was *lost*. Jesus said, "I have come to seek and to save that which is lost." We have a world filled with all kinds of lostness and brokenness. Men and women are estranged from God. They are fragmented in their relationships with one another and do not understand their authentic personhood. Jesus told various parables to describe different ways individuals could be lost, including one about a lost sheep that wandered off from the rest of the flock (Luke 15:3–7). Sometimes the lostness we experience can be aimlessness, purposelessness, meaninglessness—life without direction or guidance. Many are busy going without knowing where they are going.

Some of us are like the coin the woman dropped in Jesus' parable of the lost coin (Luke 15:8–10). This coin seemed to be lost as the result of carelessness. Many feel they are the victims of circumstances and whatever has happened is not really their fault. Environmental factors have created their situations, and they are simply caught in the web of life.

Others are lost like the prodigal son whom Jesus described in another parable (Luke 15:11–32). Their lostness is their own doing. They have rebelled, turned away from the Father, and gone to a far country to waste their lives in riotous living. There are others, though, who have a lostness like the elder brother. They are lost in self-righteousness and respectability. They see themselves as superior to other people and remain unaware that they are cut off from God.

Concern for the Whole Person

Jesus' concern for people was not limited to their soul; he was concerned with the whole person. Before you can give the bread of life to a person who is starving, you must first feed him physical bread. Before you can give someone the good news of salvation, if she is drowning, you must first rescue her from the waves. In Jesus' sermon at Nazareth, he said that the Spirit of the Lord was upon him and he had come to preach good news to the poor, heal the brokenhearted, deliver those in captivity, open the eyes of the blind, and set free the oppressed.

True evangelism—the saving message of God's grace for all persons—will also be concerned with the social conditions in which people live. Authentic evangelism will confront racism, sexism, drugs, alcoholism, war, famine, disease, child abuse, exploitation, and AIDS. All of these great social issues are concerns for evangelists. Before we can bring the good news to people, we have to be involved in working to overcome their problems.

Several years ago I watched a television program that focused on young people in our society who had run away from home. Many of them had turned to prostitution to support themselves. One of the young men who was interviewed by a reporter was asked, "Aren't you afraid of catching AIDS?" "No," he responded. "If I get it, then I'll be concerned about it." "I don't understand your attitude," the reporter frowned. "What difference does it make?" the teenager explained with despair. "I don't have anything to live for anyway."

The good news is that God loves that teen and cares for him. We, as Christians, need to reach out to all humanity with the same good news that Christ brought to people in his day. Many long to know they are loved and can begin again.

Jesus' Response to People

As we study the life of Jesus, we observe that Jesus had no set method of evangelism but responded to people where he found them and to whatever their need was. He had no rigid pattern, no Roman Road to salvation, nor did he think that there was only one way you could proclaim salvation to somebody. In his concern for humankind, he responded to each one individually. He met Nicodemus, an intelligent, scholarly, religious person who was proud of his tradition and heritage. At night on a rooftop, Jesus cut through all of Nicodemus's tradition and scholarship and declared, "You must be born again!" Works of righteousness were insufficient.

Jesus met a Samaritan woman at the village well at noon and asked for a drink of water. He cut through all of the problems and prejudices against women and Samaritans—social ostracism, sexism, racism, and false religion. He conversed with a woman who was emotional, compulsive, and unsophisticated but told her that he could give her the water of life. On one occasion Jesus was teaching in a man's home. Suddenly the straw roof was pulled apart and a man who was paralyzed was lowered through the roof to the feet of Jesus by some of his friends. Jesus looked at the man and seemingly ignored his paralysis and said to him, "Your sins are forgiven" (Luke 5:20). On another occasion an idealistic and disciplined rich young ruler came to Jesus and asked, "What good deed must I do, to have eternal life?" (Matthew 19:16). Jesus responded, "Go, sell what you possess and give to the poor, . . . and come, follow me" (Matthew 19:21). Zacchaeus had climbed up a tree to see Jesus when he passed in the village and was shocked when Jesus said to him, "I must stay at your house today" (Luke 19:5, NIV).

Jesus met people in various walks of life—a blind beggar, a demoniac, a woman caught in adultery, a mother with an ill child, a soldier with a dying slave, a leper—sinners all, and he responded to them in the situations where he met them. Jesus saw their needs and attempted to lead these persons to sense the grace, wonder, and majesty of the love of God. He had no one method. He responded to each one according to his or her need.

Jesus' Method of Teaching

Just as Jesus used variety in his response to people, so he varied the ways he used to teach the good news. When you read the Gospels, you discover that Jesus used simple, everyday experiences and stories about life to convey the good news. He drew analogies and illustrations from his listeners' home life. He spoke about bread baking in the oven, a woman sweeping the floor in search of a lost coin, candles glowing at night, farmers working in the fields, fishermen casting their nets, trees bearing both good and bad fruit, and so on. In more than fifty parables, he told simple stories related to farm life, temple life, and home life. He spoke of growing wheat, of constructing houses and building towers, and of paying taxes. He told about a son who left home with his fortune, about a shepherd and a lost sheep, and about guests at a wedding feast. All of Jesus' stories were about ordinary experiences with which his hearers could identify. Through everyday experiences and familiar analogies and figures, Jesus illustrated the good news of God's grace.

A Memorable Sentence

The Gospels are filled with simple statements of truth that Jesus used to convey his message about God. "If any one strikes you on the right cheek, turn to him the other also" (Matthew 5:39). "Seek first [God's] kingdom" (Matthew 6:33). "Do to others what you would have them do to you" (Matthew 7:12, NIV). "The greatest among you will be your servant" (Matthew 23:11, NIV). "Do not be anxious about your life. . . . Look at the birds of the air: they neither sow nor reap nor gather into barns, and yet your heavenly Father feeds them" (Matthew 6:25–26). The beatitudes and Lord's Prayer hung in listeners' minds and hearts.

Questions

Jesus often used pointed questions to arouse his listeners' interest and communicate his gospel message. "Which of you by being anxious can add a cubic to his span of life?" (Luke 12:25). "Can a blind man lead a blind man?" (Luke 6:39). He raised questions to overcome mistaken beliefs. When Jesus was accused of doing his miracles by the power of Satan, he asked, "If Satan also is divided against himself, how will his kingdom stand?" (Luke 11:18). In response to the Pharisees' question why his disciples did not fast, Jesus replied: "Can you make wedding guests fast while the bridegroom is with them?" (Luke 5:34). Sometimes Jesus directed questions to his followers to guide them in the way of the kingdom. "What is the kingdom of God like?" (Luke13:18). "If you love those who love you, what credit is that to you?" (Luke 6:32). On other occasions he asked questions to encourage his hearers to respond to his message by repenting and following him. "Who do you say that I am?" (Luke 9:20). "Why do you call me 'Lord, Lord,' and not do what I tell you?" (Luke 6:46). To the two men on the road to Emmaus, he asked: "What is this conversation which you are holding with each other as you walk?" (Luke 24:17). To Peter after his denial and Jesus' resurrection, Jesus asked: "Do you love me?" (John 21:15).

Scripture

Jesus often drew upon the Scriptures in his ministry. In his temptation experience with Satan in the wilderness, Jesus quoted passages of Scripture (Luke 4:1–12). Frequently Jesus asked his listeners, "Have you never read in the scriptures?" (see Matthew 21:42). He referred to King David's experience in the temple when he was hungry (Luke 6:3–4); the wickedness of Sodom and Gomorrah (Matthew 10:15); Jonah's three days and nights in the belly of a huge fish (Matthew 12:39–40); Abraham's presence in paradise (Luke 16:19-31); the writings of the prophets (Matthew 26:56) and psalmists (Matthew 21:42); and countless others. He accused the Sadducees of knowing "neither the scriptures nor the power of God" (Mark 12:24). To the rich young ruler, Jesus asked: "What is written in the law? How do you read?" (Luke 10:26). Jesus often used Scripture to point individuals to the presence of God and often began or ended discussions by quoting the Scriptures.

Prayerful Concern

Jesus also devoted himself to long hours of prayer. His concern and compassion for those who were lost took him to his knees. He wept over the city of Jerusalem as he approached it one day (Luke 19:41). Jerusalem was God's great center for religion, the place of his holy temple, yet the people of this city had often rejected and stoned God's prophets. Jesus continually prayed for those who had not responded to his kingdom message. He prayed before he chose his disciples, sent them out, entered a city, taught, preached, or made an important decision. He prayed for those who were like sheep without a shepherd.

Humor

On other occasions Jesus used humor to communicate his message. "How can you say, 'My friend, let me take the speck out of your eye,' when you don't see the log in your

own eye?" (Luke 6:42, CEV). "You blind leaders! You strain
out a small fly but swallow a camel" (Matthew 23:24, CEV).
Or, "It's easier for a camel to go through the eye of a needle
than for a rich person to get into God's kingdom" (Matthew
19:24, CEV). Today we often don't understand the humor in
Jesus' parables and teachings, but the people in his day
would have understood and responded with laughter.

What Methods Should We Follow Today?

What methods did Jesus use to bear the good news? He varied
them according to the people and their situations and needs.

In Mark Twain's *Huckleberry Finn,* Huck and his friend
Tom Sawyer are trying to come up with a plan to help free
old Jim, a runaway slave who has been captured and imprisoned in a cabin by Tom's uncle. Tom's imagination runs wild,
and he comes up with an elaborate plan to free Jim. It would
take years to implement the intricate plan, yet all the while
Huck and Tom are dreaming about how to set him free, Jim
is chained to his bed in a dark cabin without food and water
and is facing death. The procedure to free Jim had become
more significant than the person who needed to be rescued.

Likewise, churches may spend so much time with methods
and procedure that they never get on with the plan to rescue
those who are lost. Following the example of our Lord, we
need to be about the business of meeting people, responding
to their needs, and sharing the good news with them.

Jesus called to himself a group of disciples. First, he
trained the Twelve and a group of seventy-two to be evangelists. Then he sent them out two by two into the villages
(Luke 10:1). He told them what they might expect. Some
people would welcome them, and some would reject them.
If they were rejected, they were to shake the dust off their
feet and go on to another village.

Jesus instructed his disciples that he was sharing his mission with them. "As the Father has sent me, even so I send

you" (John 20:21). He commissioned his disciples with an unbelievable responsibility! But he also gave them a marvelous promise: "Lo, I am with you always" (Matthew 28:20). His presence and power would sustain them.

When you read the Gospel records, you will notice that Jesus Christ lived and died the message he preached. He didn't simply talk about religion and God; his whole life lived out what he taught. As John said, "The Word became flesh" (John 1:14). Jesus "emptied himself," Paul told the Philippians, "taking the form of a servant" (Philippians 2:7). It is pointless to ask how Christ emptied himself of his deity and took upon himself his humanity. It is enough to know that he sacrificially took the form of a slave to suffer and die for us. He came into our world, not that the world might minister to him, but that he might minister to others. We see in his life what our living should be—serving God by reaching out to hurting, needy people with the message of God's love and grace. Jesus didn't just talk about ministry; he lived it.

Furthermore, Jesus was willing to lay down his life so that people might know God. Jesus declared, "The Son of man . . . came not to be served, but to serve, and to give his life as a ransom for many" (Mark 10:45). "No one takes [my life] from me, but I lay it down of my own accord" (John 10:18). "I, when I am lifted up from the earth, will draw all men to myself" (John 12:32). Jesus made an astounding claim, "I am the way, and the truth, and the life; no one comes to the Father, but by me" (John 14:6). What is Jesus saying? He is telling us that it is not enough to admire him as a great teacher, to admire his wonderful miracles, to think of him as a mystical presence or as some great religious figure from the past. Jesus is saying: "I am the pathway that leads you into the presence of God. Follow my way, and I will enable you to find life."

Years ago in one of the small farming communities around Edinburgh, Scotland, a pastor visited a very distraught mother whose young daughter had run away from home and had gone to the city. The mother was afraid for her daughter and asked the pastor if there was anything he could do. He instructed the mother to get all the pictures of her daughter that she could and write on them in ink, "Come home. Love, Mother." He took the pictures and went to all the places in the city where he thought young runaway girls normally went. At each place, he left one of the pictures in a very conspicuous spot. One night the daughter walked into the living room of one of the houses and saw a picture on the mantel. She walked over to look at it and saw her own photo. On it she saw the words in her mother's own hand, "Come home. Love, Mother." She went home that night to be received into the accepting and forgiving arms of her mother.

Jesus has come extending his arms into the world to show us that God loves all people. This is our message: "Come home. Receive God's grace. Find a new beginning. God loves you. Come home."

Questions for Thought and Discussion

1. When Jesus announced that the kingdom of God was at hand, not everyone responded in a positive way. What do you think was the reason for this?

2. Jesus indicated that persons were a priority in his ministry. Discuss ways your church can follow Christ and put persons first in your ministry priorities.

3. Define what Jesus meant by the word *lost*. How is this an appropriate word to describe our present generation? What can we as a church do to guide persons out of their "lostness"?

4. Jesus demonstrated the need to be concerned not only about saving a person's soul but also about the social, economic, or cultural conditions in which that person lives. Why is it impossible to reach a person spiritually and ignore the conditions that affect this person?

5. Discuss the various methods Jesus used in his teaching. How can the church today use these methods as guidelines for its own teaching?

6. Read chapter 15 in Mark Twain's *Huckleberry Finn* where Huck and Tom Sawyer are describing a plan to free Jim, a runaway slave. Does your church sometimes become distracted or lost in plans, discussions, and procedures about evangelism and never really become involved in doing evangelism? What can you do about that lack of response?

Evan. is not "inviting people to church." Evan. is living the church.

CHAPTER 3

A *Guide*
FROM THE
Biblical
EVANGELISTS

SUPPOSE THERE HAD BEEN A TELEVISION REPORTER—LET'S say his name was Jacob Kushner—who worked for the Jerusalem Sanhedrin News Network two thousand years ago. On the evening news he reported: "On the streets of Jerusalem today, a crowd gathered around some disciples of the crucified Nazarene. People accused them of being drunk. But the spokesperson, Peter, formerly a fisherman, stood up and declared: 'It is only nine o'clock in the morning. We are not drunk. We just got up.' He told the crowd about Jesus of Nazareth, whom he said was God's Son, who did marvelous works among us. Then he was crucified and put to death. But God raised him up. Peter said that he and others were bearing witness to what they had seen and heard. He called upon the throng listening to him this morning to repent of what they had done and believe and be baptized. Unbelievably, three thousand Jews came forward and responded and now are followers of Jesus of Nazareth. Listeners, I don't know where this story is going, but you had better stay tuned!" Stay tuned indeed!

Jesus gave his disciples the commission, "Go into all the world and preach the gospel" (Mark 16:15). "You shall be my witnesses in Jerusalem . . . and to the end of the earth" (Acts 1:8). The apostle Paul later wrote, "Woe to me if I do not preach the gospel!" (1 Corinthians 9:16). The early disciples had a dramatic compulsion to share the good news of Jesus Christ.

How the Disciples Shared Their Witness

In chapter 2 we examined how Jesus modeled evangelism for us. Let us look now into the New Testament and learn from the biblical evangelists something about how they witnessed for Christ. In what ways did they share the good news?

Preaching

One way the disciples witnessed for Christ was by *preaching*. The first disciples didn't have church buildings like we do today to which they could invite people and say, "Come to our church. There is going to be preaching at eleven o'clock on Sunday morning." No, they had to preach wherever they could. Sometimes the disciples preached out of doors. Luke records many occasions in Acts where Paul, Peter, and others preached in Jerusalem, Samaria, Lystra, and a number of other places.

In Acts 2 Luke records a sermon Peter preached on the street in Jerusalem. It was likely preached outside the house where the disciples had gathered to wait for the coming of the Holy Spirit. The Jews who crowded around the disciples that day did not understand what had happened to these Christians, and Peter stood up to explain the difference in their lives (Acts 2:14–38).

One day as Peter and John walked to the temple in Jerusalem, they approached what is called the Gate Beautiful. There they met a lame beggar and healed him. After the people saw the miracle, they gathered around Peter outdoors as he proclaimed the good news of how Christ fulfilled prophecy, how he died and was raised by God. Peter called his listeners to repentance (Acts 3:12–20). On another occasion Peter preached outdoors as a crowd gathered around him after he was released from jail (Acts 5:29–32). Another of Peter's sermons was delivered to a non-Jewish crowd at the home of Cornelius, a Gentile. In a vision, God showed Peter that all persons are acceptable to God regardless of race, and he proclaimed that "everyone who believes in [Jesus] receives forgiveness of sins through his name" (Acts 10:43). Paul argued his case for Christ to the assembly of philosophers before the court of Areopagus on Mars Hill at Athens (Acts 17:16–34). Sometimes the disciples preached outdoors, wherever anybody would listen. They spoke on street corners, in the marketplace, in the city square, outside the temple, and in front of a believer's house.

On many occasions the apostles, especially Paul, began by preaching in the synagogues. Luke notes that when Paul visited a city, he would first go to the local synagogue. He did so at Damascus (Acts 9:19–20), Cyprus (13:4–5), Iconium (14:1), Thessalonica (17:1–3), and many other places. At Antioch of Pisidia, Paul and Barnabas preached in the synagogue, and they were invited to come back the next Sabbath to speak further about Christ. The following Sabbath almost the whole town came out to hear them preach (Acts 13:14–44).

Sometimes the early disciples had to defend their beliefs by preaching before religious or political leaders. On one occasion Peter and John were brought before the Sanhedrin, and Peter preached about how Christ had fulfilled prophecy and was the only one in whom salvation could be found (Acts 4:10–12). When Paul was taken before the Sanhedrin, he did the same thing (Acts 23:1–10). Paul also shared his conversion experience with the Roman officials Felix and Agrippa and preached the good news of Jesus Christ to them (Acts 24–25).

Preaching was a vital part of the ministry of Jesus' first disciples. Today our society often uses the word *preach* in a disdaining manner. "Don't preach to me," we hear people say. But the Book of Acts, which has lasted for centuries, was built around twenty-eight sermons! It is a brief sketch of the growth of the first-century church, and a major part of its contents is the digested version of twenty-eight sermons. This is a remarkable testimony to the power of preaching.

If you look carefully at Peter's first sermon and most of the rest of the sermons in Acts, you will notice they have five basic points—not three, but five! An outline for Peter's sermon and the others' might be the following: (1) "Look what Jesus did." The disciples pointed to the wonders, signs, and message of Jesus. Next they noted, (2) "Look what you did to him." This was their point if they were talking to the Jewish people. If speaking to Gentiles, they would point out how he was put to death by the Jews. To the Jews they declared, "You rejected him, crucified him and put him to death." (3) "Look what God did." God raised Jesus up from the grave. (4) "Look what we are doing." We are bearing witness to the power and glory of God. We are the witnesses to what God has done in Christ. (5) "Look what you need to do." Repent and be baptized.

When Peter preached that first sermon in Jerusalem and the Jewish people heard his message, Luke records that the listeners were cut to the heart. The word *cut* depicts an image like a surgeon who makes an incision. The truth of the message cuts like a "two-edged sword." "You must change and repent," Peter preached. The call to be baptized was strange to Jewish people, because baptism was reserved for proselytes, persons who came to Judaism from non-Jewish communities, or for somebody who had committed a gross sin and needed a radical recommitment. The message to the Jewish people was that they had committed an awful sin. They had crucified the Son of God and needed to repent and be baptized in his name. The name of Jesus represented the power of God who had raised Jesus from the dead to reign as Lord. What a powerful message this was in the first century! Preaching was indeed one of the basic formats of the apostles' witness to Christ.

Personal Witness

Another method the disciples used was *personal witness*. When Andrew talked with Jesus and believed that Jesus was the Messiah, he brought his brother Simon Peter to meet Jesus (John 1:41). After Philip met Jesus, he in turn told Nathanael about Jesus (John 1:45). The disciples were always busy telling others about Jesus. Peter and John witnessed to the lame man at the temple gate. Peter spoke to Cornelius, a Roman soldier. Paul spoke on numerous occasions to a variety of individuals—to the jailer at Philippi, to Lydia at Philippi, to the captain of the ship on which he sailed, to the Roman soldier who guarded him, and many others. Philip sharing with the Ethiopian eunuch is an excellent example of personal witnessing. The apostles did not hesitate to share their faith with other persons they met every day.

House Evangelism

The Book of Acts also shows the apostles engaging in *house-to-house visitation*. Paul said, "I did not shrink from declaring to you anything that was profitable, and teaching you in public and from house to house" (Acts 20:20). Paul spoke wherever he had opportunity, in the synagogue and from house to house. Luke said of the disciples: "Day after day, in the temple courts and from house to house, they never stopped teaching and proclaiming the good news that Jesus is the Christ" (Acts 5:42, NIV). Peter preached in the house of Cornelius, and his whole family accepted Christ (Acts 10:27–48). Paul preached in the house of Lydia, a textile saleswoman from Thyatira, and she and her household, most likely children and slaves, were baptized (Acts 16:14–15). Paul also preached in the house of the Philippian jailer, and the jailer and his family were converted and baptized (Acts 16:31–34).

The Book of Acts and Paul's epistles show that houses were often used by the early Christians as a place to gather to worship, have fellowship, hold prayer meetings, give Christian instructions, observe the Lord's Supper, and share the faith with others (2:46; 5:42; 12:12; 16:32; 18:26; 20:7; 21:7). Houses were a central focus of early Christian evangelism.

Literary Evangelism

A fourth way the early disciples spread the good news about Christ was a completely new approach we can describe as *literary evangelism*. Verses 30–31 of the twentieth chapter of John's Gospel were originally meant, most likely, as the place where he planned to end his gospel. The rest might be a long footnote. What was the purpose of the writing? John declared: "These are written that you may believe that Jesus is the Christ, the Son of God, and that by believing you may have life in his name" (v. 31, NIV).

The Gospels were a completely new way of writing in that day. As far as scholars can tell, no other groups had constructed this way of proclaiming the truth about their religious leaders. This approach was radically new. The gospel writers did not try to write a historical biography about Jesus, and therefore no single gospel contained all of the truth about Jesus Christ. In fact, John wrote, "Jesus did many other miraculous signs in the presence of his disciples, which are not recorded in this book" (20:30, NIV), and "Jesus did many other things as well. If every one of them were written down, I suppose that even the whole world would not have room for the books that would be written" (21:25, NIV).

John's Gospel, for example, does not tell us everything about Jesus. He doesn't write about Jesus' birth or baptism or about his calling the disciples, and he writes almost nothing about Jesus' ministry in Galilee. None of Jesus' parables are recorded, only seven of his miracles are mentioned, and nothing is said about the Lord's last supper with his disciples. Almost half of the gospel is devoted to Jesus' crucifixion, death, and resurrection. John did not attempt to write a biography of Jesus. His purpose was evangelistic. He wrote so people might understand who Jesus Christ was and be drawn to him.

Luke, the medical doctor, poet, and historian who wrote both a gospel and Acts, stated that his purpose in writing was that individuals might know about Jesus Christ and what God had done through him. As others who were "eyewitnesses and ministers of the word" had delivered their accounts, Luke declared, "It seemed good to me also . . . to write an orderly account for you, most excellent Theophilus, that you may know the truth concerning the things of which you have been informed" (Luke 1:1–4; cf. Acts 1:1–2). The Gospels were the textbooks the young church used to study the life and teachings of Jesus Christ. But they were also vehicles for sharing the good news of Christ with others. The epistles of Paul and others were to be heard and not just read by individuals. They were sermons that were to be read publicly to the congregations.

Most of us first came to Christ through the work of an individual. But following the work of that person, we began to read and study the Scriptures. And as we read Scripture and other biblically based books, our faith experience deepened and we gained direction for our lives.

A Closer Look at the Way the Disciples Shared Their Faith

Anywhere at Anytime

How did the biblical evangelists bear witness to Christ? The first thing I would mention is this: They shared their faith wherever they met people and with whatever opportunities they had. When Peter met the lame man at the Gate Beautiful, he shared his faith with him. When Paul was imprisoned and an earthquake shook the jail open, he witnessed to the jailer, who was afraid for his own life because he thought the prisoners had fled. As a result, the jailer and his family were converted.

Paul did not always use the same method; rather, he adapted to his circumstances. At Antioch in Pisidia, Paul spoke in the synagogue where his listeners were Jews. He spoke as a Jew and drew on their rich tradition. At Mars' Hill in Athens, where his hearers were mostly Greek philosophers, he drew on their own philosophers and writers. In Lystra, where the people were mostly pagan, Paul drew on natural religion to point his audience to God. When he was speaking before the Sanhedrin and the political authorities, he gave an apology (a defense) for the faith.

In each place and circumstance, Paul attempted to meet people where they were and to share the gospel in the most effective way that could be utilized in that moment. Paul and the other apostles realized the importance of being flexible and adaptable. Writing to the Corinthians, Paul declared that he accommodated himself to his circumstances in order to witness for Christ. "To the Jews I became as a Jew . . . ; to those under the law I became as one under the law. . . . To the weak I became weak" (1 Corinthians 9:19–23).

Through Personal Experience

Second, we also see in the Book of Acts the apostles sharing *out of their personal experience with Jesus Christ.* John wrote in his epistle, "That . . . which we have heard, which we have seen with our eyes, which we have looked upon and touched with our hands, concerning the word of life . . . we proclaim also to you" (1 John 1:1–3). They were witnesses to events they had seen and experienced, and they shared their experiences with others. The most dramatic testimony out of one's own personal experience came from Paul. When he stood before the Sanhedrin and later before Felix and

Agrippa, he told them about his conversion experience on the Damascus Road and how his life had been turned around from being a persecutor of the Christians to becoming a follower of the Nazarene. He shared out of his own personal experience what Jesus Christ had done for him. He had been a student of the rabbi Gamaliel and a zealous follower of the law, but his encounter on the Damascus Road had forever altered his life (Acts 22:1–21; 26:1–32).

With Enthusiasm

Third, the apostles shared their faith with enthusiasm. Peter and other Christians were accused of being drunk (Acts 2:13). Why? Because they were excited about their faith. And Festus accused Paul of being mad. "'You are out of your mind, Paul!' he shouted. 'Your great learning is driving you insane'" (Acts 26:24, NIV). Many accused the early Christians of being either drunk or insane. Being filled with the Spirit, the early Christians had become fools for Christ. They were excited about sharing their religion with others.

Because most of us do not want to be called fanatics, we keep our religion low key. Yet put us in a football stadium or beside a basketball court or at some other sporting event, and we'll get wild with excitement. Our enthusiasm about sharing the good news of Christ has grown cold.

In 1866 a missionary from India spoke before the general assembly of his church in Edinburgh, Scotland. While he was speaking, he fainted, and he was then taken outside to get some fresh air. When he recovered he asked, "What was I doing before I fainted? Oh, yes, I remember," he said. "I was pleading with the people to send missionaries to India. I did not finish. Take me back." "If you go back in there, you will die," they said. "Well," he said, "I'll die if I don't go back!"

As the missionary was taken back into the assembly, the crowd stood as one. "Fathers and mothers, you will not let your sons go. I spent twenty-five years in India. As a result, my health is broken. There are no stout grandsons to go? Then I will return; I'll be off tomorrow, and I'll let the heathen know that if I can't live for them, I'll die for them."

Enthusiasm is essential in sharing the message of Christ. The early Christians were on fire for their Lord. They wanted to share the good news of Christ with everyone they met.

With Courage

Fourth, the apostles were *courageous* in their witness. Even while Stephen was being stoned by the religious authorities, he bore witness to what he had experienced in Jesus Christ (Acts 6:5–7:60). While Paul held the garments of those who stoned Stephen, the blood of the first martyr somehow, I believe, began to penetrate Paul's mind and heart. When Jesus Christ confronted Paul on the Damascus Road, Paul's life was changed forever. The one who had been persecuting Christians now became persecuted. Paul was ridiculed, stoned, whipped, imprisoned, beaten, and shipwrecked. And there were many others besides Stephen and Paul who suffered and even died for the sake of the gospel.

Centuries earlier Moses had been afraid to go before Pharaoh as God's spokesman. His claim that he was "slow of speech and tongue" may have been his way of saying that his Egyptian language had become rusty since he had lived in Midian so long. More likely it was a thin, desperate excuse to avoid following God's command to go. When Moses prayed that God send someone else, God grew angry with him and told him that he *was* going. Aaron would be his spokesman, and the Lord God would teach him what to do and say. But go he would (Exodus 4:1–17).

Don't judge Moses too harshly. Jonah, Gideon, Elijah, Hosea, Jeremiah, and countless others whom God has called have been reluctant to speak for God. We join great company when at first we are afraid. But God assured them, and later the apostles and others through the centuries, that he was present to provide courage and strength. Jesus also assured his disciples that the Holy Spirit would guide them in what to say (Luke 12:11–12).

The movie *The Mission* recounts the story of Jesuit missionaries who went to the jungles of South America in the eighteenth century to share the gospel of Christ with Indians. The opening scene shows a Jesuit priest bound to a rough-hewn log cross that is floating down a river. A crown of thorns is on his brow. The wooden crucifix with its captive priest tumbles through the rock-strewn rapids until the cross bearing the priest is swept over a waterfall and plunges down two hundred feet through a roaring swirl of water. The first missionary who attempted to tell the good news of Christ to this tribe of Indians died violently at their hands. Later other Jesuit missionaries came to witness for Christ and take the place of the martyred priest. Those later efforts bore fruit. Thus, he did not die in vain.

Beginning with the first disciples who were courageous enough to stand up and proclaim the good news of what God had done in Christ, others have joined their ranks through the centuries. Why have persons been willing to suffer persecution and even death for Christ? Because they believed the truth of the message they proclaimed. The presence of their living Lord sustained them and gave them courage.

With the Scriptures

Fifth, the apostles drew on *the Scriptures* as their source of authority. On almost every occasion when they preached, Peter, Paul, Stephen, and others quoted from the Hebrew Bible, our Old Testament Scriptures. Peter made reference to a passage in Joel (Acts 2:16–21; cf. Joel 2:28–32). He also referred to Psalm 16:8-11 and 110:1. Philip helped the Ethiopian to understand what he was reading in Isaiah 53:7–8. Like Jesus, Paul would often state, "It is written . . . ," to settle an argument. Sometimes Paul, in true rabbinic style, would pile up Old Testament quotations to reinforce his point. He often would paraphrase a passage from memory.

Note especially his use of Deuteronomy 30:12-14, which he quoted in Romans 10:6-8. He felt free to apply the Scriptures to needs of his own day. In the sermons of Peter, Stephen, and Paul, one notes numerous references to the Old Testament. These men used Old Testament references to show that Jesus Christ was the Messiah, the fulfillment of their long-awaited expectations.

Today you and I not only draw on the Old Testament Scriptures, but on the New Testament as well, to share the good news we have heard and seen in Jesus Christ. They are our chief source for information, inspiration, and evangelism.

Years ago in India a native was walking down a dusty street and he found a fragment of paper. As he looked at it, he was able to read some of the words on it, but it was not complete because it was only part of a page. The words he read were: "I have come that you might have life." Someone told him that these words came from the Christians' book. He went to a mission and asked the missionary who had written these words, because he wanted to find life. Through this fragment from the Gospel of John, this man came to know Christ as Lord. The Scriptures provide a source from which we can continually learn of Christ and share the good news with others.

By Directing People to Jesus

Finally, note that the disciples *always pointed people to Jesus Christ*. They never tried to call attention to themselves. When Peter healed the crippled man at the temple gate and the crowd tried to venerate him for what he had done, he pointed them to Christ. When Paul and Barnabas healed a crippled man in Lystra, the crowd thought that Barnabas was Zeus and Paul was Hermes, because he was the messenger—the spokesman—of the gods. They wanted to offer sacrifice to them as gods. What an opportunity to be big shots in the kingdom! But when Paul and Barnabas heard what the people were saying, they cried: "Why are you doing this? We are humans just like you. Please give up all this foolishness. Turn to the living God" (Acts 14:15, CEV). Whenever the apostles were bearing witness to the faith, they were never trying to call attention to themselves, even when they were speaking out of their personal experience. Their goal was to lead persons to belief in Jesus Christ as Lord. As Paul declared, "For what we preach is not ourselves, but Jesus Christ as Lord" (2 Corinthians 4:5). Every witness needs to remember that we aren't to call attention to ourselves but to Jesus Christ, so that others might find in him redemption and eternal life.

Our Time to Witness

The pages of the New Testament are filled with individuals who shared the good news about Christ. Take a moment and read the last chapter of Paul's letter to the Roman church. Note the long list of the names of persons who were a part of the Roman church and to whom Paul wanted to be remembered. They were fellow Christians who helped him spread the faith. Now it is your turn and mine to be witnesses. The torch has been passed into your hand and mine, and we are challenged to pass on the light about God's grace. Some will let the light wane, flicker, and go out. Others, however, will carry the light courageously and enthusiastically, lifting their torches high and carrying the faith forward.

Theologian Walter Marshall Horton said that one of the finest evidences of the absolution of sin he had ever seen was given not by a priest or a minister but by a nurse in a hospital. A woman had been brought to the hospital seriously hurt from being in a drunken brawl. Doctors and nurses soon realized that there was nothing that could be done for her. As the young woman lay dying, a nurse sat by her bed to give her whatever assistance she could. The nurse looked at the dying woman's face and wondered how one so young could look so old, wrinkled, and weary.

The young woman opened her eyes and looked up at the nurse and said: "I want you to tell me something, and tell me straight. Do you think God cares about people like me? Do you think he could forgive anyone as bad as me?" The nurse hesitated for a moment and drew on all the religious resources she could muster before she responded. "I'm telling you straight," she said. "God cares about you, and he forgives you." The young woman gave a sigh and slipped into unconsciousness. As death approached, the lines on her face changed and her countenance became smoother.

You and I need to share that kind of good news with all persons, just as the disciples did centuries ago. It is now our responsibility to bear witness to Christ. Will we fail or will we succeed?

Questions for Thought and Discussion

1. List and discuss the various ways the disciples witnessed for Christ.

2. Examine Peter's sermon in Acts 2 and summarize his five-part outline. How can that outline provide a model for our teaching and preaching about Christ today?

3. The apostles shared their faith out of their personal experience with Christ. How is it possible for Christians to do that today?

4. What were some other ways the biblical evangelists shared their faith? How can modern Christians use these methods today?

5. Walter Marshall Horton tells about a nurse who spoke words of assurance and forgiveness to a dying woman. How is this evangelism? Ask others in your group to share some experience they have had in helping others experience God's forgiving love.

CHAPTER 4

The *Motive*
FOR
EVANGELISM

SEVERAL YEARS AGO FRED CRADDOCK, PROFESSOR OF NEW Testament at Candler School of Theology, Emory University, in Atlanta, Georgia, went to a victory celebration party following a University of Georgia football game. The party was held in a wealthy suburban section of Atlanta at a splendidly restored Victorian style home with a high vaulted ceiling. There were about thirty to thirty-five people present whose ages ranged from thirty to fifty. Everyone was dressed up in the kind of clothing that said, "How about them dogs!"

Dr. Craddock and his wife entered the house and didn't know anyone there other than the couple with whom they attended the game. They met the hostess, who was putting out trays of sandwiches and drinks as they entered the house.

A woman who was overly dressed, too bejeweled to have just returned from a football game, stood up and took center stage. "I think we should all sing the doxology!" she exclaimed. And before they had a chance to vote on it, she began to sing. A few people, Dr. Craddock observed, joined in and sang with gusto. Most folks studied their shoelaces; a few hummed along. Others looked for a place to set down their drink as if they didn't think they should hold it during the doxology. Dr. Craddock acknowledged that he felt a little awkward.

When they finished singing, the woman said, mostly to the men, "You can talk all you want to about the running of Herschel Walker, but it was Jesus who gave us the victory."

Somebody asked, "Do you really believe that?"

"Of course I do," she replied. "Jesus said, 'Whatever you ask in my name, I'll give it.' And I said, 'Jesus, I want us to win more than anything in the world.' And we won! And I'm not ashamed of the gospel. I'm not ashamed to say it anywhere, because Jesus said, 'Shout it from the housetops.'"

By that time Dr. Craddock and some others had moved into the kitchen. They could still hear her talking, and one of the men looked at Dr. Craddock and asked, "Do you think that woman is drunk?"

"Well, I don't know," Dr. Craddock responded. "We just moved to Georgia last year!"

The hostess had come into the kitchen and was refilling a tray. The guests had become very silent. "If that woman doesn't shut her d— mouth," the hostess said, "she's going to ruin my party!"

Dr. Craddock said that before he knew it, he said something and didn't know why he did. He asked the hostess, "Are you a Christian?"

She said, "Yes, but I don't believe in just shouting it everywhere and to everyone."

The talkative woman at a football party symbolizes a part of the problem with trying to do evangelism today. There is always some shouting in the living room and whispering in the kitchen. You have seen the TV hucksters who say that if you will write them a letter and send money, they will mail you their book or tape, which will enable you to get rich, healthy, and whatever else you want in life. Craddock reminds us that we may have seen others who have shouted in different ways. Did you hear about the weight-lifters who

THE MOTIVE FOR EVANGELISM

said that before they became Christians they were ninety-eight-pound weaklings? Jesus pumped them up and made them husky. Have you seen the advertisements that entice viewers to come watch some character who is quoting Scripture and at the same time yo-yoing with both hands? Or how about the man who was seven-feet-two-inches tall and advertised, "Before I became a Christian, I was a midget"?

When the Shouting Is Too Loud

Shouts! We hear them in all kinds of places. Some people shout in our face about what Jesus supposedly has done for them. Some of us are offended by their shouting. Their approach rubs us the wrong way, and we are embarrassed by their distortions of Christianity. These people likely do more harm than good. What has happened to those of us who do not like this "shouting?" These people have caused us to be mute. We have become silent, and we do not share the good news of Christ with anyone.

The church has always struggled with those who have shouted too loudly. The motives of these persons are mixed. Some shout simply for selfish reasons, to get attention or in an attempt to get wealthy or become famous. Some shout to increase their numbers, achieve denominational recognition, or inflate their image. Others shout out of fear. For too long we have let caricatures—false images of evangelism—keep us from doing what the church was founded to do.

Genuine Motives for Witnessing

When we read the New Testament, we discover that the disciples were filled with tremendous enthusiasm for sharing the good news of Jesus Christ. They were willing to suffer ridicule, persecution, rejection, imprisonment, and even death. The secret of their zeal and the courage for their

44

convictions rested, I believe, on five basic motives, which should still be the motivating forces for the church's evangelism today. These motives inspired the first disciples and can help us break through our silence so we will proclaim authentically the good news about Jesus Christ.

A Sense of God's Love

The first-century disciples' primary motive for evangelizing rested, I believe, in a great sense of the love of God. The disciples had experienced the power of God's grace in Jesus Christ in such a way that they were forever changed. In 2 Corinthians Paul wrote, "We are not commending ourselves" (5:12, NRSV). What Paul meant was that he was not trying to call attention to himself as he told the Corinthians about Jesus Christ. "I am not boasting of anything about my life. I am writing to you about the love of Christ." He acknowledged that apart from Christ he had been dead *in* sin. In Christ he had become dead *to* sin. His motive was not to gain anything for himself but to serve God. To some he might appear to be "beside himself," but his action was a response to the love of God in Christ.

The love of Christ controlled Paul. In 2 Corinthians 5:14 Paul writes, "For the love of Christ controls us, because we are convinced that one has died for all; therefore all have died." Note that Paul stressed that it was not his love of Christ but Christ's love of him that ruled his life. Christ's love enabled Paul to find forgiveness of his sins and to begin anew. His conscious commitment to Christ resulted in a radical change in his life.

The word "therefore" in this passage indicates a paramount change. Life in Christ has given the believer a new motive—a Christ-centered purpose. Jesus Christ gives his followers direction, power, and purpose. The disciples experienced God's love in the life, death, and resurrection of Christ. The love of Christ gave the disciples a zeal that enabled them to face danger, defeat, disappointment, and even death. The love they experienced in Christ was so vital that they wanted to tell others about it.

Do you recall the story of the resurrection appearance of Jesus to his disciples on the seashore of Tiberias? It was there he asked Peter three times, "Do you love me?" Peter replied each time, "Yes, Lord, you know I love you." "Then," Jesus said, "feed my sheep." Jesus did not ask Peter if he loved the sheep; Jesus asked instead if Peter loved him. The motive for Peter's and the other disciples' witnessing arose initially out of their awareness of Christ's profound love for them. Having experienced the love of Christ, the disciples wanted in turn to share that love with others. "We love," John wrote, "because he first loved us" (1 John 4:19).

One of the most noted Christians in Japan in the twentieth century was a man named Toyohiko Kagawa. During his days as a student and before he became a Christian, Kagawa was very ill with tuberculosis. He had been sent home from the hospital to die in his hut in a fishing village. One day there was a knock at his door, and a missionary asked permission to enter. Kagawa explained to him that he had TB and that it was very contagious. "I have come today with something more contagious than disease," the missionary said. "I have come with the love of God." The missionary came in and nursed Kagawa back to health. Later Kagawa became a Christian and was considered by many until his death in 1960 the leading Christian evangelist of Japan. The love of God he experienced through a missionary touched his life and made it forever different. He in turn touched thousands of others with this same love of God.

The disciples began sharing their faith out of a profound sense of God's love. They saw this love supremely in the God who had come uniquely into the world through his Son, who laid down his life on a cross and then rose from the grave. Their love for others originated in the love they had experienced in Christ.

A Sense of Gratitude

Second, the early believers were motivated with an over-whelming sense of gratitude for their new life in Christ. Their experience of God's marvelous love made them profoundly grateful. They served Christ not primarily because they were commanded or commissioned to do so, but out of a deep appreciation for his sacrificial love. Paul wrote, "Thanks be to God for his inexpressible gift!" (2 Corinthians 9:15). Paul had felt the crushing power of sin. The law had not been able to free him but had bound him rigidly with its demands and details. The love of God in Christ had set him free from the bondage of the law and his past sins. For that he was forever grateful.

The Lord's Supper was often referred to by early Christians as the *Eucharist*. The New Testament Greek word from which Eucharist comes is literally translated "thanksgiving." Every time the disciples gathered to celebrate the Lord's Supper, it was a time they expressed thanksgiving for God's amazing gift to them. As we gather at the Lord's Table, we do not celebrate good advice or good etiquette but the good news of God's profound love that was manifest on the cross of Christ. Can we ever be grateful enough? Our experience of love is incomplete until we express thanks.

A Sense of Grace

Third, the disciples were powerfully motivated because they had experienced an opportunity to begin again. They had been given a second chance through God's forgiving grace, and they wanted to share that good news with others.

Many people are shackled to the past and cannot free themselves from their sins and mistakes. Their sins are like chains that weigh them down and shackle them to the past. They search for release but are so burdened down by the past that they cannot get free from its hold.

You may have seen some time in the past the *Peanuts* comic strip where Linus says, "I guess it's wrong always to be worrying about tomorrow. Maybe we should think only about today." Charlie Brown replies: "No, that would be giving up. . . . I'm still hoping that yesterday will get better!"

Ah, but yesterday doesn't get better. We have to learn to walk away from it, and the only way we can do that is to experience the power of God's redeeming grace that makes us new and cleanses us from our past sins. This is Paul's great declaration in his Second Epistle to the Corinthians. "If any one is in Christ, he is a new creation" (5:17). "In Christ" was Paul's favorite definition of a Christian. In fact, he used the phrase "in Christ" fifty-five times in his epistles. To be "in Christ" means that a radical change has taken place in a person's life—so radical that Paul declared that Christ makes the person a "new creation."

The word *new* rings through the New Testament like a bell sounding the freshness and vitality of the gospel. Jesus said he came to give us "new life," "a new commandment," "a new covenant," "a new song," "new wine," and "a new heaven and a new earth." The writer of Hebrews said that Jesus was "the mediator of a new covenant" (Hebrews 9:15).

Years ago in Hyde Park in London, a communist stood addressing a crowd that had gathered around him. He pointed to a man in the crowd who was dressed very shabbily and said to him, "Communism can put a new coat on that man." A man standing nearby said, "But Christianity can put a new man in the coat." That is the radical difference Jesus Christ can make. He gives everyone an opportunity to begin again. As Paul says, "The old has passed away, behold, the new has come" (2 Corinthians 5:17).

One of the noted physicians in London of some years past was a man named A. J. Cronin. One day a young boy was brought to the hospital desperately ill with diphtheria. A tube was inserted into his throat so he could breathe, and a nurse was stationed to see that the tube remained clear. Unfortunately, she dozed off and awakened to find that the tube was blocked with mucus. Instead of cleaning the tube, she panicked and hysterically called the doctor out of sleep. When he got to the child's side, it was too late. The doctor was outraged that a child should die so needlessly and wrote out his report demanding the nurse's immediate expulsion. He called her in and read, his voice trembling with resentment, what he had written to the board of health. She stood before him in silence almost fainting with shame and remorse. "Well, have you nothing to say for yourself?" he asked. After a moment of silence, she made this stammering plea: "Give me . . . give me another chance."

The doctor was shocked. As he saw it, the nurse had failed at her responsibility, and there was nothing else to do but dismiss her. He told her to leave, sealed his report, and retired to bed, but he was unable to sleep. A far-off word floated in and continued to whisper: "Forgive us our trespasses. . . ." The next morning he tore up the report and gave the nurse another chance. Later that young nurse became the head of a large hospital and one of the most honored nurses in England.

"Give me another chance" is our plea. We raise our voices to God and cry, "Give me another opportunity," and God forgives.

The gospel of Jesus Christ tells us that no matter what your sins are, you can experience forgiveness. Look at the apostle Paul. He persecuted the first Christians, but his life was forever changed by his experience on the Damascus Road. God's grace and forgiveness forever gave Paul a great sense of gratitude for his new beginning.

A Sense of Concern

Go further with me and see if you don't agree that a fourth motivator for the early disciples was a genuine sense of concern. Paul reminded the Corinthians that Christ died for all (2 Corinthians 5:14). Throughout the New Testament, from the Gospels to the Book of Revelation, the writers point out the radical difference between those "in Christ" and those outside of him. Sin has brought a separation, an alienation, between God and humans. Jesus Christ came to bring us back from our wandering and to point us in a right direction so we can walk with God and experience meaning and purpose in our lives.

The church has not always expressed a deep concern for those outside of Christ. Think about our own indifference. Many of us have become silent, unwilling to share the good news of Christ with others. On May 31, 1792, William Carey stood before the London Assembly of Churches and begged for financial support for a new mission enterprise to the people in non-Christian nations. But their response was, "If God wants the heathen saved, he will save them." Fortunately, they recanted and formed the Baptist Missionary Society on October 2, 1792.

Baron Friedrich von Hugel, a German philosopher, once wrote, "Caring is everything; nothing matters but caring." If caring is absent from our lives, we will never reach out to other people.

We demonstrate in our society the power of caring. When we drive down two-lane roads, we often see signs that say, "Pass with care." During the time a young man or woman is away in military service, families send them "care" packages. Sometimes we request the postmaster to stamp on a package, "Handle with care." We speak about needing "tender loving care" when we feel ill or low in spirits. There is nothing more frustrating than to hear an individual say about another person or situation, "Oh, well, I really couldn't care less!"

If we don't care, we will never reach out to help another. The Greek philosopher Socrates wrote that "before any person can move the world, he must first be moved himself." You and I must be motivated by genuine concern for others if we are going to reach them for Christ.

A young boy had moved with his family into a new community and was trying to make friends with some new playmates. The other kids were playing a game of hide and seek.

The boy's father was watching nearby as the children ran off to hide. He said to his young son, "Why don't you come over here and hide behind this tree and see if they can find you here?" "But Dad," the son replied, "Suppose they really don't care!" If Christians do not care enough to search out where others are in their relationship with God, we will never help them discover the good news of Christ for themselves. We must have a profound concern about the radical difference that the new life in Christ can make for them.

A Sense of Compulsion

Notice finally that the early disciples were motivated by a great sense of compulsion. Paul said that "Christ's love compels us" (2 Corinthians 5:14, NIV). When I was a student in seminary, I had Dr. Jesse Weatherspoon for preaching. He warned us about preaching what he called "musty" sermons. These are sermons in which a preacher tells his listeners, "You *must* do this and you *must* do that." I agree with his warning against pontificating with too many "musts" in a sermon. But notice when you read the New Testament how often the word *must* echoes through the pages. Jesus said, "I *must* be about my Father's business" (Luke 2:49, KJV). "The Son of man *must* be delivered into the hands of sinful men" (Luke 24:7). "The Son of man *must* suffer many things" (Mark 8:31). "You *must* be born again" (John 3:7, NIV). Paul declared that "there is no other name under heaven . . . by which we *must* be saved" (Acts 4:12).

On another occasion Paul wrote, "Woe to me if I do not preach the gospel" (1 Corinthians 9:16). He felt a sense of urgency to preach about Christ. The Greek word for *compel* has the idea of urging on, motivating one forward. The word carries the force of a raging stream that impelled Paul forward in its raging torrent. Paul was carried forward by this force to share the news of Christ's reconciliation with humans.

Paul said that this compelling drive was not only his, but that all Christians have the urgent ministry of reconciliation

51

(2 Corinthians 5:18–20). Christ's sacrifice calls all his followers to be responsible in pointing others to him and his sacrificial way. We are to be ambassadors for Christ, carrying his message, "Be reconciled to God" (v. 20). We are commissioned by God to witness to his love. Our desire to witness is rooted in what God has done for us in Christ. Our gratitude issues in the responsibility to bear witness to our faith. Those who have experienced the "new creation" in Christ want to share their joy with others. A great compulsion moves them to speak.

Alexander Whyte was a noted preacher at St. George's Church in Edinburgh, Scotland. One day a man named Rigby came by to see him. Rigby was a commercial traveler who often visited Edinburgh on business and stayed at a local hotel. Whenever he was in town, he always invited some stranger to come with him to the church. The man he had invited on Sunday at first refused but later at Rigby's persistence came with him. The man was so overtaken by Whyte's preaching that he came back that night and silently made a commitment of faith to Jesus Christ. Rigby shared that news with Rev. Whyte.

"God bless you for telling me," Whyte said. "I thought Sunday night's sermon fell flat, and I was very depressed about it." And then Whyte said, "I didn't catch your name." "Rigby," the man said. "Rigby! Man," responded Whyte, "I have been looking for you for years." He ran back into his study and came back out with a huge stack of letters. He told him that he had letters from numerous men who told him about being invited to church by a man named Rigby. In his bundle of letters, twelve came from young men, four of whom had committed their lives to professional ministry. All of this came about because one man invited others to church.

Inviting someone to church may seem like a small thing, but it can be a part of our witness for Jesus Christ. When was the last time you invited a neighbor, a friend, or a stranger to come to church with you so that he or she might hear the good news of Christ? Each of us should feel a sense of compulsion to invite others to come hear the gospel message.

If you and I are disciples of Christ, the ministry of reconciliation has been passed into your hands and mine. We are ambassadors for Christ. We are ministers of reconciliation. Can you remember the thrills you experienced when you became a Christian? Your heart beat fast because you were excited about God's grace. Can you remember when you radiated with joy at the thought of coming to church? Now perhaps your worship has become routine. You have become apathetic and have lost the sense of the wonder and mystery of God's grace. Your vision of God's love has faded. The vision of Christ's sacrificial love needs to be reawakened in your life. You need to recapture that sense of devotion and urgency the early believers had, which carried them across wide oceans, over desert regions, into dense, dark jungles and forests, across deep rivers, up mountain ranges, into strange cities and vast countryside to share the good news of Christ with others.

You and I never know. There may be a young Saul someplace along our road of life who is waiting to be transformed into a Paul. There may be a Lydia, a Mary, or a Martha, who is waiting for someone to tell her about the love and forgiveness of Christ. There may be a young Timothy waiting for a grandmother to tell him about Christ. Conversion is still possible, but the good news of Christ must be shared with other persons if they are to know God's love. We cannot keep it to ourselves.

When I was a young teenager, I attended a church training mission week at Massenetta Springs, Virginia. The preacher for the assembly was J. Winston Pearce. He concluded his sermon that day with this story. "I had come to church early one Sunday morning," he said. "About 9:15 a knock came on the door of my study. I said, 'Come in.' Luke Webb, our janitor, came into my office, and I asked him, 'What is it, Luke?' 'Dr. Pearce, Miss Kent say if you ain't gonna use de world,' as he pointed to a globe in my study, 'let the young people have it dis mawning.'" Dr. Pearce said that he told Luke that would be fine. Luke then picked up the globe firmly in his hands and carried it to the young people.

"That experience," Dr. Pearce said, "well-nigh wrecked my sermon that morning!" The words echoed in his head, "If you ain't gonna use de world, let the young people have it."

The responsibility to share this good news of Christ with others is now in your hands and mine. May the power of Christ motivate you and me to get on with the ministry of reconciliation.

Questions for Thought and Discussion

1. When have you been offended or embarrassed by someone's depiction of the Christian faith? Share what some of these depictions are.

2. Do you think it does more harm than good for someone to stand up in a ballpark with a sign reading "John 3:16"? Will that sign change any lives? Why or why not?

3. The primary motive the first-century disciples had for evangelizing was a strong sense of God's love. What modern ways of showing God's love might attract others to Christ today? Give some examples you have seen.

4. What is your reaction to the woman who had failed in her nursing responsibility and asked Dr. Cronin for a second chance? Have you met persons who are longing for a new beginning? Can you share how Christ can provide that new life for them? Practice with those in your group what you would say.

5. Do you believe that you and your church have a genuine sense of "compulsion" to witness for Christ? If not, what has caused this desire to wane? What can be done to reactivate it?

CHAPTER 5

The *Task* OF the CHURCH

A NUMBER OF YEARS AGO THE ARCHBISHOP OF CANTERBURY wrote a circular letter to his priests and asked if they would meet him in London for a "quiet day." One of his priests wrote back, "What my church needs is not a quiet day but an earthquake!"

A lot of churches today need an earthquake. Christ's Great Commission found in Matthew 28:18–20 has shaken the church like an earthquake down through the centuries. It has continuously reminded the church of its task, its missionary purpose, and its call to evangelism.

Jesus gave this commission after he had been raised from the dead. The eleven disciples had gathered to meet Jesus at a mountain to which he had directed them. There they worshiped him. Then he told them their responsibility and their missionary task. This charge has echoed through the heart of the church through the centuries. Listen to its message for us today.

THE TASK OF THE CHURCH

A Tremendous Claim

Jesus began with a *tremendous claim*. He said, "All authority in heaven and on earth has been given to me" (Matthew 28:18). Who would make such a stupendous claim? Wasn't this the Galilean peasant, the man who worked until he was thirty as a carpenter in Nazareth? Wasn't he the one who said that he didn't even have a place to put his head down at night? Wasn't he just a penniless, itinerant preacher? Where were his armies? His political power? His wealth?

Yet Jesus claimed to have all authority in heaven and on earth, the same kind of authority he taught his followers to pray for in the Lord's Prayer when he said to pray that God's will would "be done on earth as it is in heaven." He claimed that this authority had been placed in his hands by his Father.

This claim resounds throughout the New Testament. Paul wrote that the risen, glorified Christ is seated at the right hand of the Father in heavenly places and is "far above all rule and authority and power and dominion, and above every name that is named, not only in this age but also in that which is to come; and he has put all things under his feet" (Ephesians 1:21–22). In another place he wrote that Jesus is "designated Son of God in power according to the Spirit of holiness by his resurrection from the dead" (Romans 1:4). When Jesus was raised from the dead, his disciples sensed something about his power that they had not realized before the crucifixion. "Christ . . . emptied himself, taking the form of a servant. . . . he humbled himself and became obedient unto death, even death on a cross. Therefore God has highly exalted him and bestowed on him the name which is above every name, that at the name of Jesus every knee should bow, in heaven and on earth and under the earth, and every tongue confess that Jesus Christ is Lord, to the glory of God the Father" (Philippians 2:7–11). "He is before all things, and in him all things hold together" (Colossians 1:17).

Peter wrote in his first epistle, "Through him you have confidence in God, who raised him up from the dead and gave him glory" (1 Peter 1:21). The writer of the Epistle to the Hebrews declared, "We see Jesus, who for a little while was made lower than the angels, crowned with glory and honor because of the suffering of death" (Hebrews 2:9). The host of heaven worship saying, "Worthy is the Lamb who was slain, to receive power and wisdom and might and honor and glory and blessing!" (Revelation 5:12). The Scriptures affirm that this Jesus Christ is the one to whom all authority has been given. His resurrection was the sign and mark of the approval of God on his ministry.

What territorial rights does Jesus have? Of what or whom is Jesus Lord? Jesus claims all. When he stands before the door of a person's heart and knocks, he expects that individual to give him all of his or her life. This Lord, having been obedient unto death and having been raised from the grave by God, reigns triumphantly and now comes to us and challenges us to follow him and his way. Jesus demands control of the material, mental, and moral areas of our life.

People down through the ages have given Christ authority and power in their lives. Kings have knelt and taken their oath in his name. Presidents in our country lay their hands on a Bible and pledge their oath in his name. Rulers have gone forth under the banner of his cross to claim new territories. Others have given their lives in sacrifice to spread his good news around the world. Hospitals, universities, homes for children and the elderly have been established under his authority. Artists, writers, poets, musicians, architects, scientists—those in every realm of life—have been touched by his authority. No area is free from his influence.

Christ knocks at the door of every person's life. Unfortunately, many are like the poor woman who could not pay her rent. One day she heard knocking at her door. The knocking grew louder, but she continued to ignore it. Later when her pastor, who had come with money to pay her rent, asked why

she had not responded, she said she thought it was the land-
lord who had come to collect the rent money. She did not realize that the one who was knocking had come to pay her rent.

Likewise, some people draw back when they hear Christ
knocking at their heart's door, for they fear that his summons
is a call to pay the rent. Jesus, however, has come to give
them a gift—redemption. He comes not demanding a pay-
ment but to deliver the good news that he has already paid
for their redemption through his sacrificial death. His sacrifice draws people to himself, and he summons them to
respond to his call to discipleship.

Two thousand years ago a restless and depressed man
named Matthew was seen leaning over his tax ledger. He had
been rejected by his friends because he was a Jew who collected taxes from his Jewish friends and neighbors for the
Roman government. On this day a shadow fell across his
table. He looked up and recognized that the shadow was cast
by Jesus of Nazareth. He had heard this preacher before and
had been deeply moved by him. But could he, a tax collector
who was despised and rejected by his own Jewish people,
find a new beginning? Then Jesus said to him, "Come, follow
me." The man who later authored one of the Gospels laid
down his tax ledger, got up, and followed Jesus Christ. His
life was forever changed.

Jesus Christ made an audacious claim. "All authority in
heaven and on earth has been given to me." He knocks at
your heart and mine, and you and I must determine how
we will respond.

A Great Commission

Go a step further with me as we look at Matthew 28:18–20,
and you will see that Jesus not only makes a tremendous
claim, but also gives the church a *great commission*. Here he
presents to us our task or responsibility as his church. Jesus
says in verses 19–20, "Go therefore and make disciples of all

nations, baptizing them in the name of the Father and of the Son and of the Holy Spirit, and teaching them to observe all that I have commanded you." The principle action here is "make disciples." The going, baptizing, and teaching are subordinate to making disciples. Literally this passage reads, "As you are going, as you are baptizing, as you are teaching, you will make disciples." You will be discipling persons who will commit their lives to the authority of Jesus and will learn and grow under his teachings.

Several summers ago my family rented a place at the beach. We discovered that one of the problems you can have at a beach cottage is ants. Something sweet was accidentally dropped on the floor in the kitchen, a message went forth, and soon a whole host of ants had gathered around that savory item. When I saw the ants gathered there with their long line extended from their home base, I thought about the church. Why can't we, with such a marvelous message, go forth and share that great news with others? Shouldn't there be a signal going out to those around the church to come and savor the good news of the gospel? Let us be about that business.

Disciple All Nations

Jesus said, "Disciple all nations." "All" indicates the wide horizon of the evangelistic message of Christ. Christ is concerned with all persons, classes, ages, races, and sexes. Paul writes in Ephesians about the dividing wall that separated Jews and Gentiles in the temple. The Jewish temple was composed of a series of courts beginning with the exterior Court of the Gentiles, followed by the Court of the Women, then the Court of the Israelites for the men, the Court of the Priests, and finally the Holy of Holies. Paul declared that the death of Jesus had broken down all of these dividing walls. Christ brought an end to barriers, and people could come directly to God.

Unfortunately, many walls still exist today, barriers between classes, nations, genders, and races. But in Christ, we can have peace and unity, for he broke down all of these

59

walls. Jesus' message is one of inclusiveness. Jew or Greek, barbarian or intellectual, cultured or uncouth, male or female, rich or poor, young or old, conqueror or conquered, white or black, red or yellow, slave or free—all persons are welcome in Christ's kingdom. The commission to disciple all nations reminds us of the unlimited horizon of the Christian church. Christ extends his love to all persons.

In the Andes Mountains on the border of Argentina and Chile there stands a huge bronze statue of Christ. The statue was made out of metal from discarded guns and cannons. At the base of the statue these words are inscribed: "Sooner shall these mountains crumble into dust than Argentines and Chileans break the peace that they have sworn to maintain at the feet of Christ the Redeemer." At the feet of Christ the Redeemer, persons of all races can meet. The arms of Jesus Christ are extended to them in love, forgiveness, and acceptance.

Baptize the Believers

The next part of Jesus' commission was, "baptizing them in the name of the Father and of the Son and of the Holy Spirit." "Name" stands for person. Being baptized in someone's name means that you now belong to them. You are bought with a price and are now God's property.

This passage contains one of the earliest references to the Trinity. Being baptized in the name of the Father, Son, and Holy Spirit symbolizes the all-encompassing nature of the triune God we worship. A baptized Christian is like a glass submerged in water. Water fills the inside of the glass and surrounds the outside as well. Likewise, we are both filled with God's Spirit and surrounded by God's presence. When we are baptized, we are surrounded by the reality of God's presence as Creator, Redeemer, and Spirit. To recognize God as Creator is to affirm God as the one who creates and sustains life. As the incarnate Son, he makes us whole. As Spirit, he guides and directs our lives.

Teach the Believers

Jesus also commissioned his followers to go into the world "teaching." When you make disciples, they must constantly be taught, because continuous education is essential to growth in grace. Jesus didn't say to make disciples and let them stay where they entered the kingdom. Instead, he commissioned us to "teach" them. The church is charged to develop those whom they have evangelized into mature Christians. This requires instruction, pastoral nurture, worship, fellowship, and prayer.

The primary emphasis is on teaching obedience to Jesus' commandments. The emphasis is not on teaching a creed but on teaching conduct, not on teaching something to be believed but on teaching something to be done. For Jesus said, ". . . teaching them *to observe* all that I have commanded you."

Recently my wife, Emily, and I spent the night at Shakertown in Pleasant Hill, Kentucky. Shakertown is the site where a small sect called Shakers settled when they migrated to America from England during the colonial period. Their name was given to them by observers who noted their religious practice of shaking vigorously during worship to rid their body of sins. Shakers believed in hard work, stringent living, and efficient methods of labor. Therefore, their farms prospered.

The Shakers practiced celibacy, and if a family converted to the Shakers, the family had to split up, with the women and girls living on one side of the "dorm" and men and boys on the other. Only minimal dialogue took place between the sexes. Since Shakers did not marry and two-thirds of the children left when they became adults, their only option for growth as a sect was through conversion of visitors who came to the meeting house to watch the Shakers sing and shake in worship. The minister observed them from a small window upstairs and came down after the service was over and talked with anyone who indicated interest in joining them. The number of Shakers continued to decrease until the last surviving Shaker at Pleasant Hill died in 1903.

Some of the unique Shaker architecture, furniture, and songs have survived. Their faith, however, died because they failed to pass it on. A cloistered faith, shut off from the outside world, cannot reach others. This danger is always with the church. We may have majestic buildings, lovely furnishings, beautiful hymns, and elegant sermons, but if we do not share our faith with others outside our buildings, we may, like the Shakers, leave empty buildings and lovely furniture without passing on our faith.

Christ Promises His Presence

A Continuous Presence

Go with me further into this text and note that Jesus has given us his *continuous presence.* He said, "Lo, I am with you always, to the close of the age." Here we find first his *personal presence:* "I am with you." I *am* echoes through the Gospel of John, where Jesus said, "I am the light of the world"; "I am the bread of life"; "I am the true vine"; "I am the way, the truth, and the life"; "I am the resurrection and the life"; "Before Abraham was I am"; "I am the good shepherd"; "I am the door to the sheep." I *am* in this passage indicates Jesus' continuous presence with us.

Marc Lovelace was a professor of archaeology whom I studied under at Southeastern Baptist Seminary at Wake Forest, North Carolina. He gave an interesting interpretation of the passage in Exodus 3 where God responded to Moses' question, "If I come to the people of Israel and say to them, 'The God of your fathers has sent me to you,' and they ask me, 'What is his name?' what shall I say to them?" God's reply was: "I AM WHO I AM." Dr. Lovelace said that on some ancient tablets that had recently been unearthed and deciphered, the Hebrew could be translated "I SPEAK" as well as "I AM." "Tell them that I who speak sent you." This emphasis stresses that God not only is, but that God communicates with us. Jesus Christ is not only one who was, but he is here now. We are able to feel his power today and are able to communicate continuously with him.

An Abiding Presence

Jesus is also an *abiding presence.* "Lo, I am with you *always."* "All the days" is a literal translation of this word. Jesus is present with us not only on good days but on bad days as well— when we are happy or sad, sorrowful or joyful, suffering or healthy. God is with us whether our faith is weak or strong, whether we feel close to God or have questions and doubts. No matter where we are in life's pilgrimage, God is with us.

Years ago I traveled several miles up a mountain road in heavy fog to a church one Sunday morning. I could hardly see the road at times. Occasionally I had to stop the car and get out to see if I was still on the road. As I got closer to the top of the mountain, light began to flicker through the fog. When I reached the top of the mountain, the fog dissipated and light flooded my car and my spirit. That experience became a parable of life for me. It helped me to remember that even on the darkest, foggiest day God is there. We cannot always see the sun on a foggy day, but we know that it is still shining. God is present whether we feel his presence or not.

A Triumphant Presence

Finally, Jesus said, "Lo, I am with you always, *to the close of the age."* Jesus is a *triumphant presence.* We are not sure how history will end, but the Bible teaches that God is in control. Christ will triumph. Jesus is depicted in Scripture as a conquering Lord who will sit in final judgment on history. He will be present to the close of the age.

I heard several years ago about some missionaries who were visiting in a Muslim city. While they were there, it came time for the Muslim call to prayer. A crier climbed to the top of the wall, stood up, and cried, "There is but one

God, and he is Allah, and Mohammed is his prophet." The words echoed around the walls of the city. As the words finished bouncing around the walls, the missionary could stand it no longer. Finally, he cupped his hands and began to yell, "There is but one God, and he is Jehovah. And he has but one Son, and he is Jesus Christ, Lord of lords, and King of kings." These words began to echo around the wall of the city. The missionary's young son tugged on his sleeve and said, "Daddy, they just can't stop it, can they?"

The church proclaims boldly that Jesus Christ is Lord of lords and King of kings. Having made a tremendous claim of authority, Jesus has given his church a great commission. To share the good news of Christ is your task and mine as members of Christ's church. The continuous presence of Christ will inspire, strengthen, motivate, and guide our witness for him.

Questions for Thought and Discussion

1. Why is it still the responsibility of the church to challenge persons to live under the authority of Christ today? Is it possible? How?

2. Discuss the meaning of the Greek verb meaning *disciple.* Note that going, baptizing, and teaching are subordinate to making disciples.

3. Discuss what happened to the Shakers in Pleasant Hill, Kentucky, because they refused to pass on their beliefs by active evangelism. Could this be a danger for your church?

4. Ask yourself whether your church emphasis is mostly on your own interests, comforts, pleasures, budget, and building rather than on passing on the faith.

5. Share with one another how you believe Christ can be a continuous, abiding, and triumphant presence today. What will Christ's presence enable the church to do?

CHAPTER 6

Sharing
Your Faith
WITH
OTHERS

*T*HE FRONT COVER OF *TIME* MAGAZINE IN MAY OF 1940 featured the picture of a very courageous German pastor named Martin Niemoller. The photo caption read, "In Germany the cross has not bowed to the Swastika." Niemoller had preached a famous sermon entitled "God Is My Fuhrer." Because of his opposition to Hitler, he was imprisoned for eight years. After he had been in prison for about four years, he had a dream one night in which he saw Hitler standing before the judgment bar of God and declaring that he had not heard the gospel. "In my dream," Niemoller said, "I heard the voice of God directed toward me inquiring, 'Were you not with him one whole hour and did not tell him about my Son?' " When Niemoller awakened from his dream, he realized that he had indeed had such an opportunity to speak to Adolf Hitler and had done nothing. From that moment onward, Niemoller began to share the gospel of Christ with the guards and other persons with whom he came in contact in the Nazi prison.

Reluctant Witness

Sometimes the most difficult door for an evangelist to open is the door to his or her own heart. Often we are reluctant to share the good news of Christ with others. In fact, we even avoid opportunities. Let us look at some of the reasons for our reluctance.

"I'm Afraid"

Sometimes we are simply afraid—and rightly so, when we look back in history and realize how many persons suffered and died to witness for Christ. John the Baptist preached repentance because the kingdom of God was coming, and for that he was put to death. Jesus was crucified. Stephen, Paul, and most of the disciples likely died violent deaths. And on down through the ages many who have witnessed for Christ have been persecuted and put to death. But few of us in this country face that kind of danger today. We are more afraid of being rejected, ridiculed, criticized, embarrassed, or misunderstood or of being incompetent or offensive. If, however, we are gracious and respectful, most people will receive us well.

"I'm Too Old (or Too Young)"

Some are reluctant to evangelize because they feel that age is a factor. "I'm too young" or "I'm too old," they claim. But God called Abraham to found a new nation when he was an old man. And even though Jeremiah protested that he was too young, God called him to bear his message to the nation of Israel. A. T. Robertson speculated that Paul was probably fifty when he began his work as a missionary and most likely died when he was about sixty-five.[1] No one would say that Paul was an old man when he began his work, but he was certainly beyond the age range when persons are appointed for such work by mission boards today. Some of the finest persons I have ever known who are faithful witnesses for

Christ have been elderly people. I remember a Sunday school teacher in his seventies who continued to teach twelve-year-old boys in Sunday school. The boys loved him, and his influence stayed with them for the rest of their lives. He was a powerful witness to the gospel.

"I'm Theologically Inadequate"

Some Christians are reluctant to evangelize because they feel theologically inadequate. Many laypersons declare, "I am not a theologian. Who am I to talk to others?" We are all on pilgrimage in our faith. Even the most profound theologian has not arrived spiritually. But you do not have to be a trained theologian to witness for Christ. You should use every opportunity to be better trained and equipped to share your faith. The most important thing, however, is not your theological astuteness but your concern and love for people.

"I'm a New Christian"

Some people are reluctant witnesses on the grounds that they have not been a Christian long enough. Yet often the most powerful witnesses for Christ are new believers. Immediately after Andrew talked with Jesus, he went and brought his brother, Simon Peter, to meet Jesus. After Philip committed himself to Jesus, he brought Nathanael to him. The New Testament is filled with accounts of newly converted Christians telling others about their newfound faith. New Christians are still excited about their experience and want others to hear about it.

"I'm Not Spiritual Enough"

Others say, "I'm not spiritual enough to witness to others. I might not know exactly what to say." I don't know exactly how we measure the spiritual life of a person, but all of us feel spiritually inadequate. We are all human vessels subject to weaknesses, but God has and continues to use all kinds of people in his service.

SHARING YOUR FAITH WITH OTHERS

A man used to poke fun at himself as he would visit in the homes of people for his church. He would say, "My friends would be surprised if they could see me visiting now. They know that my wife and I stopped going to church for about twenty years. We realized that something was missing in our lives and started going back. One night I was asked to speak in prayer meeting. I told them what the church meant to us now and about the strength we received from it. And now here I am out trying to tell others about what Jesus means to us." Maybe the best measure of spiritual depth is concern and love.

"It's the Minister's Job"

Many have said that they don't witness because that is the pastor's or ministerial staff's job. They are the ones we pay to do the witnessing for our church. Of course the pastor and other ministerial staff should be doing some of the witnessing, but the New Testament clearly says that it is the responsibility of every Christian to share the good news of Jesus Christ with others. If we leave all of the witnessing to the professional ministers, that limits evangelism to a small group of persons.

One of the most dedicated laypersons in my congregation was a man whose name was Lewis Wayne. When I was making preparation for Mr. Wayne's funeral service, I had an opportunity to talk with one of his sons who is a Baptist minister in Virginia. Bob told me that he learned how to witness to others from his father. Bob worked for a while with his father in the service station he owned. He watched his father talk to customers about what Jesus Christ and his church meant to him while he worked on their cars. Bob learned from his father—a layperson—how to share the faith.

"I Don't Have the Time"

Still others protest, "I just don't have time to witness." Well, people come across your path every day wherever you are.

You will have many opportunities without going out of your way. Furthermore, we always make time for what is important to us. The average American spends thirty-five hours a week watching TV. How about giving up some of that time? Everyone is busy, but we have to be willing to give priority time to witnessing.

"People Are Not Interested"

Others use the excuse, "People aren't interested in spiritual matters." That is just not true. At the root of many personal problems is a hunger for God and a desire to find spiritual direction. When a natural disaster, such as a flood, fire, or hurricane occurs, a person is often pushed to the depths of his or her being to know why such things happen and take innocent lives and destroy valuable property. The terrorist attacks on the World Trade Towers in New York and on the Pentagon provoked nationwide discussions about the nature of God, of evil, of justice, of forgiveness, and of life itself. Even less devastating life events, such as weddings, divorces, funerals, births, and graduations, bring people to critical points of questioning spiritual realities, and as Christians, we need to be sensitive to those circumstances and to the individuals involved in them, seeking opportunity as providence and relationships allow to minister the healing and renewing message of the gospel.

Philip: A Model for Witnessing

Let us look for a moment at the model for witnessing we find in the encounter of Philip with the Ethiopian eunuch (Acts 8:26–40). Remember that Philip was a layperson, one of the seven set apart by the early church as a deacon to dispense aid to the poor. He was a Hellenist, which meant that he was a Greek-speaking Jew, who most likely was foreign born. He had left Jerusalem during the persecution that followed the death of Stephen, and he was the first preacher of the gospel to go to Samaria. While he was in Samaria, a populous city, God's Spirit directed him to an isolated road to talk with a single individual.

On this lonely desert road south of Jerusalem toward Gaza, Philip met an Ethiopian eunuch who was the secretary of the treasury of the Candace dynasty. Scholars have debated exactly who this man was. I think he was a black man from Ethiopia who had undergone physical surgery to become a eunuch. This procedure was often done to persons who were willing to serve in a high position in the official court of the ancient governments of Egypt or Ethiopia. The Ethiopian most likely belonged to a group called the God-fearers. His physical mutilation had denied him the opportunity to become a Jewish proselyte. He had probably been worshiping in Jerusalem and was returning home. By focusing on an Ethiopian eunuch, Luke is proclaiming vividly the wideness of the gospel story.

The Spirit's Guidance

Look first at the guidance of the Holy Spirit. God's Spirit reached out to Philip in a large city in Samaria, where he would have numerous opportunities to witness, yet made this request: "I want you to go now to Gaza and preach over on the roadside to one individual." We read in Acts 6:3 that Philip was a man "full of the Spirit." He had committed his life to God and was open and responsive to God. Hearing God's command, Philip obeyed. I don't know exactly how he experienced the Spirit's guidance, but I don't think Luke was referring to a miracle so much as a feeling within. God's Spirit may have directed Philip as God directs you and me. I have sometimes had a feeling, as I'm sure you have, to go see someone. Philip may have had a similar feeling.

In some ways this may have seemed like a chance meeting, especially to the Ethiopian man. But God's Spirit often works through such "chance" meetings. Like Philip, we may discover that being obedient to God's Spirit may lead us into unfamiliar situations, but God's Spirit, nevertheless, will inspire, equip, and empower us to work for him.

Philip's Responsiveness

Second, Philip was responsive. He responded to the man where he found him. He, like the Ethiopian, was most likely riding in his chariot when they met on the Gaza Road. As the custom was in ancient times, travelers would greet each other and sometimes talk awhile. Traveling in isolated places like the Gaza desert, they were always glad to see a fellow traveler. He used the opportunity he had.

Philip's Guidance

Third, Philip attempted to guide and instruct the Ethiopian. The Ethiopian had been reading from the Book of Isaiah. How did Philip know what the man was reading? He most likely was reading aloud, and Philip heard the text he was reading. Philip expressed interest by asking a question: "Do you understand what you are reading?" The Ethiopian responded, "How can I unless somebody will guide me?" Philip responded to the man's request by starting where the man was. He didn't tell him about where he had been or what he had accomplished. He didn't tell the man where he wished the man was spiritually. He met the man where he was. He began with the passage of Scripture the man was reading and helped him to interpret it.

Don't you wish you could know what Philip said? Luke says that Philip took this passage of Scripture and preached Jesus to him. He helped him to see that the passage in Isaiah was a prophecy that was fulfilled in Jesus Christ, that Jesus was the long-awaited Messiah.

The Ethiopian's Response

Now notice the response of the Ethiopian. He halted his chariot. He and Philip likely had been riding along together for many hours. The words "he commanded the chariot to stop" (Acts 8:38) carry a symbolic truth as well as a literal meaning. When Jesus Christ comes into our lives, he stops us, turns us around, and sends us in a new direction.

After stopping the carriage, the Ethiopian said, "See, here is water! What is to prevent my being baptized?" That was a very significant question. Since the Ethiopian was a eunuch, he had been prevented from being a proselyte to Judaism (see Deut. 23:1), but Philip and the eunuch "went down into the water" (v. 38), and the eunuch was baptized into Christ.

A Revolutionary Result

By recording this account of Philip and the Ethiopian, Luke was making a revolutionary statement about the power of the gospel to include all persons in God's grace. The gospel of Jesus Christ had broken out of Judaism and had gone into Samaria, where a black eunuch had become a Christian and was baptized. On that isolated desert road, the gospel burst all the old bonds of Jewish restriction and accepted any person as a brother or sister who trusted Jesus as Lord. When we let God's Spirit guide us, we never know where and to whom he may take us with his message of love.

Some Guidelines for Witnessing

With the story of Philip and the Ethiopian eunuch as our backdrop, let us look at some basic guidelines for witnessing to others about the good news of Christ.

Live a Christlike Example

First, you must live your life as a Christlike example. None of us is ever truly a perfect Christian example. Nevertheless, Jesus said, "I have given you an example, that you also should do as I have done to you" (John 13:15). Paul wrote about the believers, "You . . . are our letter of recommendation, written on your hearts, to be known and read by all men" (2 Corinthians 3:2). You and I can't say something with our lips and expect people to believe it if our lives deny it. We are, as Luther said, "little Christs to others." If we are going to witness for Christ, we have to live a life that is Christlike. The most powerful witness we may ever have for Christ is a "presence," or a way of life, that radiates a Christlikeness that draws others to our Lord. Through words of encouragement, affirmation, support, concern, and a personal winsomeness, others may "overhear" the gospel and be drawn to the Lord we follow.

I conducted a funeral service for a committed Christian recently. I had talked with this man and his wife on several occasions as he was slowly dying of cancer. He had met his illness courageously, and both he and his wife had talked openly about his illness and death. They spent some marvelous time each day in meditation together and spent long hours reflecting about their life. They also spent meaningful time with their children and grandchildren.

Following this man's funeral service, his son-in-law came up to me and said, "I am not a Christian, but witnessing the life of my father-in-law, I want to give my life to Christ. Anybody who could live and die like he did has something I want." Later I baptized this man. He became a Christian because of the example of his father-in-law.

Try Some Simple Things

Second, there are simple things you can do all the time to share the good news with others. You can invite non-Christians to your Sunday school class, to church, or to some special program your church is sponsoring, such as youth activities, a Christian concert or film, or a Christmas or Easter service. You can share a book, an article, or copies of your pastor's sermons or tapes with others. You will never know what a difference these simple things can make in the life of another person until you do them.

Roy M. Oswald and Speed B. Leas of the Alban Institute, writing in *The Inviting Church,* relate the results of a survey of newcomers in twenty-two congregations of many denominations in Indianapolis, Philadelphia, and Atlanta. In response to the question, "What brought you to church?" the survey noted that 2 percent saw an advertisement, 6 percent were invited by the pastor, 6 percent came through an organized evangelistic outreach, and 86 percent came because of an invitation from a friend or relative.[2] The strongest factor in reaching people was personal, informal invitation. Studies by church growth advocates like Donald McGavran and George Hunter agree that personal contact, or "contagious evangelism," is still the most effective means for church growth.[3] Do not sell short the affect of your personal invitation. It may be a powerful first step in evangelism.

A young man is attending seminary and preparing for ministry today because one of the teenagers in our church invited him to church. He had never gone to church until he was invited by his friend. After a few months of coming to Sunday school and church, he made a profession of faith. He committed his life to Christ and was baptized. Later he felt a call into the ministry, and today he is in college preparing to be a minister. All because a teenage friend invited him to come to church.

Listen to People

Third, you can listen to what people are saying to you. Everyone has a history, and we need to listen to the histories of others—their pains, aches, frustrations, hurts, needs, and tears as well as their dreams, hopes, longings, and goals. As you listen to people, opportunities will arise naturally for you to share something with them about Christ, his love, and his church.

A woman once said to a friend who had listened to her for months, "Since you have listened to my struggles for so long, I will listen to you now. Tell me about the difference Jesus

Christ has made in your life." Listening can open the door to the heart and mind. Listening shows that you care and genuinely want to understand.

Share Your Spiritual Story

Fourth, you can share your spiritual story with non-Christians. Delos Miles says that every person has a spiritual autobiography and a testimony.[4] Some persons have put their spiritual autobiography into a book like C. S. Lewis's *Surprised by Joy*, Sam Shoemaker's *I Stand by the Door*, John Claypool's *Opening Blind Eyes*, Elton Trueblood's *While It Is Day*, or Frederick Buechner's *The Sacred Journey*. Books like these are spiritual autobiographies that relay in book form a person's spiritual pilgrimage. As Christians, we all have a spiritual autobiography. You may never put it in book form, but you can share it verbally with another.

Your testimony is a brief clipping from your longer spiritual autobiography. In your testimony you describe how you became a Christian and what Jesus Christ means to you now. In telling your story, you do not attempt to call attention to yourself but to point people to Christ.

A Clipping from My Spiritual Story

When I was a teenager, I was, like many teenagers, interested primarily in athletics and recreation. I really didn't care much for school. I would sit in the back row most of the time and read books. I loved to read but was not interested in school subjects. I felt there was something missing in my life, but I didn't know what it was. My parents had encouraged my brother, sister, and me to go to Sunday school. I would go sometimes, but most of the time I would simply walk around. My parents thought I was in Sunday school, but I was mostly walking and thinking.

At this time, I was very interested in Boy Scouting and spent a lot of weekends camping and hiking. When I went before the district board of review for my Eagle Scout Award, I was asked as we concluded: "Have you ever thought about working on the God and Country Award?" "No, to be honest," I said, "I haven't." Someone gave me a little pamphlet about the badge, but I really wasn't very interested in working on it because it was related to church. And church certainly didn't turn me on.

Later I began to think more about getting that award. I had become an Eagle Scout, and I thought that the new badge would look nice on my shirt. But as I read the material, I soon realized that I would have to go to church and Sunday school because many of the requirements were church related. I started attending Sunday school regularly and going to youth meetings. I even joined the youth choir, attended youth fellowships, assisted at special functions, and went faithfully to worship services. I also had to read my Bible and other literature. After I had done all this for a while, God's Spirit began to work through these activities and through people at church to confront me with my need of Christ. I soon realized that I had a vacuum in my life without him.

At one morning service, I stepped forward with several others to commit my life to Jesus Christ as Lord. I began to follow him and study more about him. My life was different; I now had direction, meaning, and purpose. My conversion was not dramatic, but it was a deliberate choice I made as a sixteen-year-old boy. I began to work harder in the church, and the next year, when I was seventeen, I was asked to be the youth week pastor. The first sermon I ever preached was entitled "A Discovery of the Real Jesus." I tried to describe what Jesus had meant to my life since I surrendered it to him. Soon I sensed a call into the ministry. My life was turned around by that experience, never to be the same again.

I had the wrong motive to begin with in that I was primarily interested in getting a scouting award. But God uses all kinds of means to touch our lives. He works patiently through our good or bad intentions to reach us. I know today that my life is radically different and richly blessed because of the strength I feel from God's daily presence.

You have a story too. You can tell what your life was like before you became a Christian, how you came to know your need of Christ, how you became a Christian, and how your life is different today.

Share the Gospel Story

A fifth guideline for witnessing is to tell the gospel story. As a teenager, I was given a book by E. Y. Mullins entitled *Talks on Soul Winning.* Mullins was one of the first presidents of the Southern Baptist Theological Seminary in Louisville, Kentucky. This book offers some lessons that provide structure for witnessing to our faith. One practical tool I learned is called the Roman Road. By using passages from the Book of Romans, one can guide a non-Christian down the roadway to becoming a Christian. You begin with, "All have sinned and fall short of the glory of God" (Romans 3:23). Next you tell them, "God shows his love for us in that while we were yet sinners Christ died for us" (Romans 5:8). Then you indicate their response in Romans 10:9, "If you confess with your lips that Jesus is Lord and believe in your heart that God raised him from the dead, you will be saved."

If you prefer, you can turn to the Gospel of John and take another approach. First, you note Jesus' relationship to God the Father: "In the beginning was the Word, and the Word was with God, and the Word was God" (John 1:1). Second, you stress our human need: "No one can see the kingdom of God unless he is born again" (John 3:3, NIV). And then you speak about God's provision to meet our need: "God so loved the world that he gave his only Son, that whoever believes in him should not perish but have eternal life" (John 3:16).

Another way you might keep the simple facts of the gospel story in your mind is by focusing on the 3 Rs. First, you talk about the *ruin* in our lives—how we are lost without Christ. Sin has separated us from God, others, and our authentic self. Second, tell about God's great *redemption*. You can speak about Christ's sacrifice on the cross and the costly nature of God's grace. Third, note the *response* that Christ calls from us. He asks us to respond in faith by committing our lives to him.

We have to be careful, however, that our guidelines don't become gadgets. That is, the process must not become more important than the goal. Nevertheless, I believe we all need some formula to enable us to keep the biblical message clearly before us. Whatever you use, share the message of God's love naturally. If people can see that the gospel is meaningful to you, they will listen and respond better.

A young minister had a very wealthy member in his church. She attended faithfully, but her husband never came with her. He became very concerned about the woman's husband. One day the minister went by the man's office and asked if he could talk with him for a few moments. The wealthy man said that would be fine. The minister sat down and very simply shared with him the gospel story. When he finished, he said to the man: "I think you ought to do something about this one way or the other." The man didn't say a word. He just sat there.

The minister felt very uncomfortable, but he went through the gospel story again. When he finished this time, there still was not a sound. The minister felt so uncomfortable that he wanted to get up and leave. Then the man reached over and got a pad and scribbled a few words on it and slid it over to him. "I am so deeply moved that I cannot speak." This was the first time anybody had ever told him the gospel story in an adult, straightforward manner. He gave his life to Christ and became a dedicated member of that church.[5]

People are hungry to hear the message of God's love. So you and I need to share this message with them and invite them to respond. After you have shared your spiritual story or the gospel story, you can ask questions such as this: "Would you like to have direction in your life?" "Have you ever thought about the difference that Christ has made in my life and the difference he can make in yours?" "Have you found peace with God?" "Have you experienced the forgiving love of God?"

Respect the other person's opinions. Allow him or her to talk, and be sure to listen. Be natural, tactful, sincere, and patient, and do not argue. Be positive. Plant the gospel seed and leave the rest to the Holy Spirit. We cannot drag people into the kingdom of God. Only God's Spirit can convert them.

Share Hospitality

Sometimes we can open a spiritual door through table fellowship. This is as simple as inviting someone for coffee or a meal in your home or a restaurant. Over coffee or a meal, the conversation might move to spiritual concerns. A layperson in my church who goes to Taiwan for business told how a mealtime discussion with other businesspeople eventually turned to whether or not he believed in God. At that meal and on several other occasions, he has shared his faith with people who have been very interested and responsive. You don't have to go across the ocean to share a meal and your witness. You can go next door, across town, or wherever the opportunity arises.

David and Ana D'Amico presently serve as "missionaries" to the United Nations diplomatic community in New York City. Much of their ministry is done through hospitality evangelism. They invite diplomats from around the world into their apartment for desert or a meal, and these occasions open the door for discussing spiritual matters. They meet these persons with friendship, concern, attention, and a listening ear, and often they have an opportunity to share their faith. Wherever we live we can share our faith through hospitality.

Look Again at Philip

Look with me again at Philip. What happened to Philip after he witnessed to the Ethiopian eunuch? Acts 8:40 indicates that he went to Caesarea. Then for twenty years we don't hear anything about him. When Paul visited Caesarea twenty years later, he went to the home of Philip, who now had four daughters who were prophesying—preaching in the church (Acts 21:8–9). In his own quiet way, Philip had served God faithfully for twenty years. He continued to witness to his own family and others. You can do the same.

Edward Kimball was a dry goods salesman in Boston. He also taught a Sunday school class in the Mount Vernon Congregational Church. He was concerned about a young man in his Sunday school class who was not a Christian and decided to go down to the store where the young man worked as a shoe salesman and talk to him about Christ.

As he approached the store, he wondered if he should visit during business hours. He didn't want to embarrass the young man. "Suppose after I have gone, the other clerks begin to ask the boy who I am and taunt him because his Sunday school teacher came to see him to make him a good boy." He was so preoccupied with his thoughts that he walked past the store. But he turned around and decided to go in and talk to the young man. He found the young man all alone in the back of the store wrapping and stacking shoes. Kimball put his hand on the young man's shoulder and said, "I want you to give your life to Christ, who loves you and wants your love." That day Dwight L. Moody committed his life to Christ because a layperson cared enough to share the good news of Christ with him.[6]

There are many ways to witness for Christ. Discover your way. But remember, God has called all of us as Christians to speak a good word about Christ to others. Like our Lord, let us be about our Father's business.

Notes

1. A. T. Robertson, *Epochs in the Life of Paul* (Nashville: Broadman, 1976), 11.

2. Roy M. Oswald and Speed B. Leas, *The Inviting Church* (Washington, D.C.: The Alban Institute, 1987), 44.

3. George G. Hunter, *The Contagious Congregation* (Nashville: Abingdon, 1979); and Donald McGavran, *Understanding Church Growth* (Grand Rapids: Eerdmans, 1980).

4. Delos Miles, *Introduction to Evangelism* (Nashville: Broadman, 1983), 161ff.

5. George Buttrick, ed., "The Acts of the Apostles," *The Interpreter's Bible,* vol. 9 (New York: Abingdon-Cokesbury, 1965), 117.

6. J. C. Pollock, *Moody: A Biographical Portrait of the Pacesetter in Modern Evangelism* (New York: Macmillan, 1963).

Questions for Thought and Discussion

1. List and discuss some reasons Christians are often reluctant to share the good news of Christ with others.

2. Use Philip as a role model for witnessing. What are some lessons the Christian witness might draw from Philip?

3. I shared five guidelines for witnessing. Assign different guidelines to persons in your group. Ask them to come prepared to discuss, raise questions, and give examples for their particular guideline.

4. I gave a "clipping" from my spiritual story as an example of a way to witness. Ask those in your group to share a "clipping" from their own spiritual story and evaluate its role in witnessing. Note its strengths and weaknesses.

5. Suggest various ways a believer might share the gospel story. How effective do you believe the Roman Road approach, the Gospel of John approach, the 3 Rs approach, or other approaches are in reaching people for Christ today?

6. How do we witness to the faith and not turn guidelines into gadgets? Are there new models that could communicate the gospel more effectively with contemporary persons? Discuss them.

7. There is no one way to witness for Christ. Some persons have used table fellowship, concerts, recreation, retreats, puppet shows, films, seeker services, and so on to witness to those outside the faith. What are some other ways to witness to unbelievers?

CHAPTER 7

Evangelism:
Journey INWARD,
Journey OUTWARD

THE CHURCH IS COMPOSED OF PERSONS WHO HAVE
committed their lives to the lordship of Jesus Christ.
We enter the church through the door of conversion and
embark on a journey as disciples of Christ. Within the
church, believers are nurtured in our knowledge of God and
strengthened to follow Christ's way. But we are also aware
that the church is the only organization in the world that
does not exist solely for the sake of its own members. The
church has been established not so that you and I can have a
place to go for fellowship or entertainment or even for having our particular needs met, but for the purpose of equipping us to share the gospel of Jesus Christ with others. The
church was founded to be the agent of reconciliation
between God and humans. Thus, our purpose as members of
the church is to advance that reconciling work.

Journey Inward

The Christian life is a journey, ushering us from our entrance
into the church through commitment to Jesus Christ
through our continuing growth as his disciples, rendering

EVANGELISM: JOURNEY INWARD, JOURNEY OUTWARD

service and witness along the way. The journey sometimes leads through valleys of despondency, difficulty, struggle, illness, and grief. At other times we stand on mountaintops of vibrant faith and clear vision concerning the purpose and direction of our journey. Wherever our journey takes us, we may always travel with the assurance that we are not alone, for the Lord goes before us to show us the way.

The Journey Begins

Like any journey, the Christian pilgrimage has a beginning. Our point of origin emerges from that particular moment when we gave our lives in faith to Christ. No one sets foot on the Christian pathway without that initial commitment. The early Christians often were called men and women of "The Way" because they followed the One who said "I am the way, and the truth, and the life" (John 14:6). Christ is the one who beckons us to step out on his way.

Personal Religious Experience

We place our feet on the Christian pathway to begin a vital personal experience with Christ. No one else can make this personal commitment for us; it cannot be done by proxy. It is a personal decision each person must make to begin the journey as a believer.

The New Testament refers to this initial spiritual step variously as conversion (Acts 3:19), new birth (John 3:3), belief (Acts 16:31), and being saved (Acts 2:47), to cite just a few biblical images. Our faith is personal and we testify as the early disciples did, "I know whom I have believed" (2 Timothy 1:12). Remember the scene where Jesus stood before Pilate and Pilate asked, "Are you the king of the Jews?" Jesus' response was to ask Pilate, "Are you asking this on your own or did someone tell you about me?" (John 18:34, CEV). That should be our question, too, shouldn't it? Is our faith experience our own, or is it second-hand knowledge we learned from another? By confessing our sins, repenting of them, and trusting by faith in the Lord, we receive the redemption, grace, and forgiveness of God. Out of that personal experience we become men and women of "The Way."

Variety of Doorways

We are not all required to have the same kind of conversion experience. Each of us may encounter God in a different way. For some, the experience may be highly emotional; others may respond calmly out of years of faithful church and Bible school attendance. Still others may take the path of a more reasoned faith to overcome their doubts or fears, while some may respond out of a radical sense of relief from the heavy burden of their sins. Some may meet Christ at their business as Matthew did, at the marketplace like the woman at the well (John 4:3–30), in their homes as Lydia did (Acts 16:13–15), in affliction as blind Bartimaeus did (Mark 10:46), or unexpectedly as Paul did (Acts 26:12–20). God's Spirit moves in the hearts of men and women in ways beyond our understanding or explanation.

A person who grew up in the church and one who has never walked in the door would likely not have a similar conversion experience. A child's experience will most likely be drastically different from a young adult's or that of an elderly person. Look around any church and observe the people in the pews. An individual's age, personality, occupation, sex, race, and so on may suggest or conceal a special conversion experience. For each one, however, that experience is uniquely personal and meaningful.

Directions for the Journey

Once we put our foot on the path of faith, we seek to receive directions from the one who is the Way and who is our guide along the way. Our journey takes on purpose as we get our directions, guidance, perspective, and meaning from Christ. "I came," Jesus told us, "that everyone would have life, and have it in its fullest" (John 10:10, CEV). This does not mean that we will never have doubts, fears, questions, struggles, grief, or problems. But the assurance that Christ is always with us, no matter what the circumstances of life might be, will strengthen us to face whatever crosses our pathway. Knowing that nothing separates us from the love of God sustains us and gives us courage (Romans 8:37–39).

One of my church members said to me one day as she was slowly dying with cancer, "Pastor, no matter how deep I sink in pain or suffering, I thank God that he is deeper still to hold me up." Whether we are walking in the sunlight or in the darkness of despair, our Lord is there to guide us along the way. The words of the angel to the women who sought Jesus at his tomb assure us today: "I know that you seek Jesus who was crucified. He is not here. . . . he is going before you" (Matthew 28:5–6). Our Lord goes before us to lead the way. We follow with confidence.

Learning along the Way

The followers who committed their lives to Jesus were called disciples. Disciples were "learners"—individuals seeking to grow in their knowledge, awareness, and truth of the Master's teachings. The Gospels are a result of the careful listening and responses of some of these disciples. The writers of the Gospels wanted others to learn about the life, death, teachings, and resurrection of Jesus Christ. They had learned from him and passed his story and message on for others to hear.

Beyond Selfishness

Our central sin is self-centeredness or pride. It is what Reinhold Niebuhr has called "God almightiness"—the attempt to be God and see all of life through our lens of selfishness. This truth was made apparent to me again recently in a bumper sticker I saw. It read: "Born Right the First Time." This view asserts that we do not need to change. We are okay at birth. But our encounter with

Christ has revealed to us our sinfulness, especially our self-centeredness, and our need to find forgiveness for our sins and an opportunity to begin again. Christ calls us to come out of our selfishness and move to a higher way. Our motto is not "me first," nor is our focus only on self-preservation. When our life focuses on self, we have difficulty seeing beyond our own immediate needs or desires. Jesus declares that we find meaning and purpose in life paradoxically by losing our life in something beyond self-interest. "For whoever would save his life will lose it; and whoever loses his life for my sake, he will save it" (Luke 9:24). In committing our lives to something—to Someone—beyond our self and selfishness, we forget about ourselves. As we follow Christ, we find that we save ourselves in dedicating ourselves to some cause beyond ourselves and receive only as we give.

Albert Schweitzer, the noted theologian, organist, and professor, thought that something was missing in his life. He decided to go and serve as a medical missionary to Lambaréné, Africa, to acknowledge to God the blessings he had received. "I must not accept this happiness as a matter of course," Schweitzer wrote in his autobiography, "but must give something in return for it. . . . I tried to settle what meaning lay hidden for me in the saying of Jesus: 'Whosoever would save his life shall lose it, and whosoever shall lose his life for my sake shall save it' . . . In addition to the outward, I now had inward happiness."[1]

One of our first steps on this inward journey is to receive from Christ's presence the strength and inner resources we need to break free from the shackles of selfishness. Then we will begin to walk life's pathway focusing not on self-centered goals but on worthy causes that aid others along the way. Christ lifts our vision to see the needs of others and to discern how we can assist them. Jesus reveals to us that self-centeredness only leads to a dead-end street, but we follow *him* with the assurance that his way of service is indeed going somewhere.

Personal Equipment for the Journey

An essential part of a Christian's equipment for the inner spiritual journey is personal and corporate *worship*. Worship, according to the Christian tradition, is not optional; it is something a Christian is compelled to do. A Christian worships if he or she really cares about God. Worship sustains us, and without it, we die spiritually. Worship is not an occasional matter; it needs to be practiced on a continuous basis. It is as essential as light is for seeing, sound for hearing, and air for breathing.

Corporate worship becomes a weekly focus of the individual mind and heart with a community of believers on the power and presence of God. The word *sabbath* is derived from an old Babylonian word that means "stop doing what you normally do." Corporate worship enables us to find an oasis in time when we can adore, praise, express thanksgiving, and receive the assurance of God's love, forgiveness, and grace. We gather to confess our sins, acknowledge our vulnerability, express our gratitude, and sense God's grace and power.

A Christian also grows spiritually by personal or private *devotion*. By setting apart a quiet time each day, or some particular time on a regular basis, a Christian opens his or her mind to the presence of Christ. During this time, you might read passages from the Bible; for example, a selection from the Old Testament and the New Testament. Meditate on the text. Use a commentary to glean insights into the meaning of the passage. You might want to keep a notebook and jot down any thoughts, ideas, prayers, questions, or longings that are prompted by your reading.

You might also choose to read some devotional material from various writers. On my personal list, I read faithfully from the writings of Harry Emerson Fosdick, Leslie Weatherhead, C. S. Lewis, John Killinger, Walter Rauschenbusch, John Baillie, and others. Their words often motivate my thinking or expand my understanding of God. Then I spend some time in quiet refection and prayer, focusing on God's greatness, confessing my sins, accepting God's forgiveness and grace, and simply being still and trying to listen for God's voice. Sometimes I take a walk in the woods or around the block, or I sit by a stream or a fountain in a park or in some quiet place away from people.

One of my spiritual models is John Baillie, who was a Scottish theologian and principal of New College at the University of Edinburgh. Three objects in his study symbolized his faith and ministry. One was the desk at which he did his theological writing, the second was a chair where he did his reading, and the third was a cushion near a window and bookcase where he would kneel, meditate, and pray. This great theologian knew the importance of developing the inner life and never assumed that he did not need to spend quiet time in worship before God.

The Path before Us

Our inward journey on the Christian pathway is never complete; we do not reach a final destination in our faith growth. The path is ever before us, beckoning us on to an even higher way of spiritual insight. No one can ever "arrive" spiritually and assume that there is no further need for spiritual knowledge. Who would even have the audacity to declare that he or she has all the knowledge one can possibly have about God? We are always in the process of growing to be more like Christ. Jesus has challenged his followers to "be perfect, therefore, as your Father in heaven is perfect" (Matthew 5:48, NIV). Our spiritual growth will always come up short when measured by that divine standard.

As disciples of Christ, we strive always to be open to God's Spirit in order to grow in our awareness of God. We never graduate from the spiritual university but are returning students, open to the teachings of Christ and to the presence and power of God. We open ourselves to our Master Teacher, so that we might be continuously advancing in our knowledge of the Christian way and in new ways to serve our Lord. As disciple-learners we remain open to learn more from our Teacher as we travel along the Way. We share with others along the way what we have learned, and we learn from others as well, constantly acknowledging our desire to learn even more in order to be like our Lord.

Motivation along Life's Journey

As we continue our spiritual journey, we are often motivated by various factors. Some of our motivation may arise externally—from the needs we see in persons along the way, or from causes that lift us out of our self-centeredness into service, or from a desire to deepen our own spiritual life, or by a profound need in our own life. Alternatively, we may be motivated out of a sense of profound personal relief for the forgiveness of our own sins or by a deep sense of gratitude for God's grace.

Motivated to Thanksgiving

Just as the early disciples were motivated to follow their Lord out of a sense of gratitude for God's love and forgiveness, so we travel along the Way with a strong sense of thanksgiving for all we have experienced in Christ and for all we know we will receive as we continue the journey. As we began our journey, gratitude rose to our lips as we reflected on God's forgiveness of our sins. Along the way, we may pause to thank God for strength to overcome temptation, for recovery from illness, for the encouragement of a friend, for the strength to face the loss of a loved one, for the birth of a child or a grandchild, for the gift of life itself, and for many other events.

Too, doxology rises to our lips as we look all around us and rejoice at the wonder of God's creation—of the splendor in a sunset or sunrise, of the beauty of the changing seasons, of the majestic mountains and immense oceans, of the minute detail of a tiny seashell or a fragile spider web. The mystery of the natural world around us and of the heavens above us often causes us to pause and reflect on God's gift of life to us and on the potential for growth in the awesome world in which we live.

Karl Barth, the noted German theologian, has observed that all theology ultimately arises from gratitude. Our sense of gratitude for all that God has done for us colors all our thinking about God and our understanding of God's revelation to us through creation, Christ, and the Scriptures. As we look inward and outward on our spiritual journey, we need to pause again and again to express our thankfulness to God for all our blessings.

Motivated to Transformation

Our inner growth with Christ as we follow him as a disciple should be reflected in the kind of life we live daily. If we have been born again—converted—then our actions should indicate this change in all we do. Jesus said, "You will know them [my disciples] by their fruits" (Matthew 7:16). Paul declared in Romans 6:4, "We were buried with him [Christ] by baptism into death, so that . . . we too might walk in newness of life." It was observed of the early Christians how they loved one another. As Christians, our love for our fellow believers and for others ought to be evidence of our transformed life within.

Jesus modeled acceptance and forgiveness to many people who were despised and rejected by even the religious leaders of his day. Jesus reached out to a tax collector such as Zacchaeus and even called Matthew to be one of his disciples. He befriended the poor and the rich, men and women, old and young, the Israelites and Gentiles. He extended his concern and grace to the hurting persons he met—to the diseased, the blind, the lame, and the deaf. He assured all those he met that they were persons of worth and that God loved them and was concerned about their every need.

As we follow our Lord, we seek to emulate his style and show respect, forgiveness, love, and acceptance of others. Jesus even challenged us to love those who hurt us (Matthew 5:44)—not an easy thing to do. But our Lord demonstrated the extent of his willingness to follow his own teaching by forgiving his enemies from the cross and by challenging his disciples to share the message of God's inclusive love to all the world. Our understanding of the inclusive love of God will bring down barriers between individuals, races, sexes, and nations.

James has reminded us that faith without works is dead (James 2:18). Even "God so loved the world that he gave . . ."! It is not enough to talk about our experience with Christ and the change he has transformed in us. Our lives, if we have had a genuine experience with Christ, will demonstrate that change in all we say and do.

Motivated to Serve Christ and Share the Good News

Our conversion experience with Christ turns us away from self-centeredness and places our feet on the way of service and sacrifice. By "losing" our life in service for Christ, we discover the true meaning of life. Our understanding of service arises out of Christ as our model, guide, standard, and example. His life and teachings point us to escaping our selfishness and to assisting others in need. The challenge to serve others or to share the gospel with others may not always come at a convenient time or place, nor will it always have a simple solution or a pat answer. Those we help or those with whom we share the good news may not always understand our motives or good intentions, nor thank us for our words or assistance. But this should not deter us or inhibit our willingness to minister to them, sharing the gospel in word and deed. As the opportunity arises, just as our Lord responded to the persons who reached out to him for help as he traveled among them, we too must respond to their need with the good news of the gospel.

Recently an opportunity came unexpectedly into my life. I was comfortably sitting at home one night reading, watching television, and enjoying the fire in the fireplace when I was called to the telephone and informed by a woman at one of the hospitals that a certain male patient would like for me to come visit. She gave me his name, and I said I would come by tomorrow and see him. I wrote the name down and looked it up in the church directory, because the woman had indicated that he was a church member. The name was unfamiliar to me, but that was not a surprise, because there are numerous times I go to the hospital to visit people whom I do not know in our large church. But I could find no listing of this person in our directory. I thought to myself, *Well, maybe he thinks he's a member. He attends church and has come long enough to think he has become a member by osmosis.*

I sat down and started reading again, and an hour or so later the phone rang once more. This time it was a nurse calling. She said, "Mr. Smith has been expecting you to come see him and has become rather disturbed that you have not come yet. Maybe," she continued, "you could talk with him by telephone." "I'm sorry. I didn't realize he wanted me to come tonight," I said. "Tell him I will be there in a few minutes." I drove to the hospital as quickly as I could. I walked into his hospital room and saw a person I didn't know. In a few minutes of conversation, this individual shared with me his own personal struggle with his fear of death and his desire to become a Christian. Unexpectedly, I had an opportunity to listen to this man's deep needs and fears and to share the good news of Christ with him. In the quietness of that hospital room, he gave his life in faith to Christ. The next day I went back and talked further with this stranger who had reached out to me at night. He may never come to our church, but in a moment of need he gave his life to Christ.

Where do you share the good news? Everywhere— everywhere there is an occasion to do it naturally. How do you do it? You do it with the gifts you have. You share through your personality, your understanding of people, and your relationship to them.

Journey Outward

Authentic evangelism takes us on a journey inward that causes us to look deep within our own lives. But we must also journey outward to meet others where they are at. To witness effectively to our faith, we must be prepared to deal with the social factors that affect people's lives. Jesus' good news message, especially as illustrated at the Nazareth synagogue, reaches out to touch people wherever they are with the social aspects of the gospel.

Unfortunately, many Christians emphasize one aspect of the gospel or the other—evangelism or social action. Some believe you can lead people on an inward journey and ignore their outward conditions. In his book *The Secular Congregation*, Robert Raines calls this the "pietist-secularist" controversy. The church-centered pietist prays, "Lord, change me." The secularist, who is world-centered, prays, "Lord, change the world."[2] Elton Trueblood, in his book *The New Man for Our Time*, reflects on the same problem. For him the polarities are the "pietist" and the "activist." The pietist always stresses the devotional life, prayer, and personal worship, while the activist is concerned about being involved in social causes. Trueblood is convinced that the answer is not either/or but both. "Serving without devotion is rootless; devotion without service is fruitless."[3]

In her book *Journey Inward, Journey Outward*, Elizabeth O'Connor has emphasized the necessity of both sides if the authentic gospel is to be proclaimed. "Renewal cannot come to the church," she believes, "unless its people are on an inward journey. It holds with equal emphasis that renewal cannot come to the church unless its people are on an outward journey."[4] It is essential to develop the inward spiritual nature, but the church is under obligation also to reach out to meet the needs of people.

Anyone can take a one-cause approach toward life. What have you done recently for your local school, or the Wishing Well Society, the Blue Cross Club, the Kentucky Horse Farm, the African Braille Society, or countless other lesser known groups? Ernest Campbell, formerly minister at the Riverside Church in New York City, told about a young student who approached him one day and asked him if he could come to a civil rights rally at ten o'clock that night. Dr. Campbell told him that he couldn't come. He had been actively involved in many causes dealing with racial issues, but this time was not convenient for him. That young man began to tongue-lash him and question his commitment. "To restore some balance in the conversation," Dr. Campbell said, "I asked him what he had done for the orphans in Hong Kong lately."

It is easy to pour all our passion into one cause and lose sight of others worthy of our interest and support. Too often we view life only from the perspective of our one cause. A wider perspective is essential to communicate the whole gospel. Some people say the church's sole purpose is soul winning. That is without question, but if it is authentically the New Testament church, it is also concerned about the social needs of people. A part of our mission is to reach out and touch people in need wherever they are in society.

Social Concern

The gospel is a two-sided coin. On one side is imprinted evangelism, and on the other side is the stamp of social action. Jesus Christ came into the world to bring wholeness into the lives of people. Therefore, the gospel is concerned with the personal needs of people and not just with their souls.

Sometimes you can't reach people for Christ unless you first minister to their social needs. When missionaries go to foreign lands to spread the gospel, they want to take the Scriptures to the natives. Thus, the Scriptures have to be translated into the language of the people by scholars. But then they may discover that most of the people can't read. So somebody has to teach them how to read. At the same time, doctors are needed to heal the people's diseases and agriculturists are needed to teach them how to farm. So, to this one country, missionaries may go as doctors, nurses, teachers, Bible translators, and agriculturists, as well as pastors or evangelists.

The church is not perpetuated just by meeting individual needs. It has to be concerned also with the deep-rooted social needs of people. When God appeared to Moses, he did not say to him, "Go to Egypt and save the souls of the Israelites." He called him to go and release them from slavery. It's hard to bring a word about salvation to a person who is starving to death. First you may have to feed him. Evangelism and social action are intertwined. We can't have one without the other and have the whole gospel message.

Social Activism

Many of the world's great social activists have been deeply committed to Jesus Christ. William Tuke, who founded the first mental hospital, was a devout Christian. John Greenleaf Whittier, who wrote some of our magnificent hymns, was repelled by slavery and worked to overcome its evil. William Booth became concerned about the poverty in London and founded the Salvation Army to minister to the poor. Albert Schweitzer went to Africa as a medical doctor to bring healing to people in a remote part of the world. God calls the church to use all kinds of avenues to spread divine love. We must provide a community where people within and without the fellowship can experience care and support.

Race Relations

Richard Armstrong shares an experience he had while serving on a board of directors of a local civic association in a predominantly Jewish community in Philadelphia. When the board expressed concern about property values dropping if black families moved into the neighborhood, Armstrong submitted a resolution calling on the board to take a strong stand for open housing and extending a welcome to all persons regardless of race, nationality, or creed. After his motion was made, a member of a neighboring church was overheard to say, "We have ways to get rid of him."

At the end of a heated discussion, Armstrong stood and made this closing statement: "I do not see how anyone can in good conscience oppose the spirit of this resolution. If it is not passed, I shall tender my resignation from this board and publicly announce my reasons." The motion passed, and integration came to the last bastion of segregation in Philadelphia.

When the meeting was over, one of the directors came up to Dr. Armstrong and said: "Dr. Armstrong, I'm a Jew, but if I decide to become a Christian, I'd join your church, because I admire the stand you and your congregation have taken on race relations."

The commitment of this congregation to being an inclusive church helped not only to set the tone and pace for the Oak Lane community of Philadelphia but opened the door to ministering with persons of all races and beliefs. Armstrong's sensitivity to the rights of minorities paved the way to enable others, who otherwise might not listen, to hear the message of evangelism.[5]

Support Groups

Another avenue for reaching people may be through special support groups that meet in your church building or other places in your community. For example, our pastoral care center has support groups for divorced persons, for those experiencing grief, for cancer victims, for family members of Alzheimer's patients, for parents of teenagers, and for others. All of these groups meet in our church building, and many of the persons who draw on these support groups are not members of our church. They come because they have a need and they have heard our church say, "We want to help you."

Other support groups might focus on men's or women's needs, sexual abuse victims, alcohol or drug addiction, children of alcoholics, or codependency. People in these groups are seeking a "safe place." The church building may be that sanctuary, or they may find it safer to meet in someone's home or in some other building. These persons long for acceptance, and nonthreatening support groups can become avenues to lead them to experience God's love, healing, and wholeness—salvation.

Concern for the Total Person

The gospel of Christ is not concerned only with individual souls but with the total person and his or her material needs. The true gospel is neither the proclamation of abstract religiosity nor of shallow good works. It cuts across all barriers to reach persons with sensitivity, discernment, and love, understanding that human beings are complex creatures of physical, emotional, psychological, and spiritual needs. We must strive to keep those concerns in balance as we seek to minister to the people around us.

Walter Rauschenbusch was a great exponent of the application of the gospel to social concerns, yet he acknowledged, "The ABC of social renewal and moral advance is for each of us to face our sins sincerely and get on a basis of frankness with God and ourselves. Therefore Christianity set out with a call for personal repentance."[6]

• • •

Let us covenant individually and as church members to be evangelists for Christ. This journey will take us inward as we grow in our personal faith, but it will also lead us outward to share the wider scope of the mission of Christ with a hurting society. Don't choose only one side of the gospel. Proclaim both, and commit to developing your own inward journey even as you reach out to minister to the needs of others.

Notes

1. Albert Schweitzer, *Out of My Life and Thought,* transl. C. T. Compton (New York: Holt, Rinehart and Winston, Inc., 1961), 85.

2. Robert Raines, *The Secular Congregation* (New York: Harper & Row, 1968), 3ff.

3. Elton Trueblood, *The New Man for Our Time* (New York: Harper & Row, 1970), 25.

4. Elizabeth O'Connor, *Journey Inward, Journey Outward* (New York: Harper & Row, 1968), 9.

5. Richard Stoll Armstrong, *The Pastoral Evangelist in the Parish* (Louisville: Westminster/John Knox, 1990), 208–9.

6. Walter Rauschenbusch, *The Social Principles of Jesus* (New York: Association Press, 1918), 8.

Questions for Thought and Discussion

1. Ask members of the group to share their personal conversion experience, and note the variety of ways in which persons have begun their Christian journey.

2. Ask the group what resources they use in their own devotional time. Allow time to discuss the various books or other resources that persons cite as being influential in their spiritual growth.

3. Do we witness to the faith only when it is convenient or whenever an opportunity arises? I gave several examples—one was from a hospital call I received late one night. React to these examples. Share some experiences of your own.

4. Ask for individuals' reactions to Elton Trueblood's quote, "Serving without devotion is rootless; devotion without service is fruitless."

5. Discuss whether you agree with the writer's conclusion that the church has to be concerned about the whole person, including personal and social needs, as well as with the salvation of that person's soul.

6. What do race relations, social activism, support groups, pastoral counseling centers, youth clubs, tutoring programs, food and clothing closets, and other ministries proclaim to a community about the message of the Christian gospel? Discuss how your church already offers some social ministries or how it might develop some new social programs to meet specific human needs in your community.

CHAPTER 8

The Difficulty of *Beginning* AT THE BEGINNING

As we talked about his faith journey, the man said to me, "I mean to begin again." But how do we begin a second time? Is it possible to get back to our starting place and step out anew? Isn't this the promise of Jesus in the "new birth"? The New Testament concepts of repentance, conversion, and regeneration all proclaim this possibility. When you and I respond to the call of Christ to follow him, this is an opportunity to begin again. Our spiritual journey begins in a personal commitment of faith to Jesus Christ as Lord, but for each of us, this new beginning looks different. We each enter the spiritual journey in a different way and at different times.

And it is also sometimes difficult for Christians to talk to others about how they can begin again. We often find ourselves tongue-tied, or moving from one foot to the other, or looking at our watch to avoid eye contact, or seeking a way to escape. This doesn't mean that we don't love Christ; we are just afraid to speak about our experience with Christ.

Paul's Experience

I have found the way the apostle Paul was so willing to share his story very helpful to me in learning to witness to my own story. We can learn how to help others find the point of beginning again by noting how Paul did it in the Book of Acts. (See especially Acts 9:1–19; 22:5–16; 26:12–18.)

When the apostle Paul spoke about his faith, he often began at the beginning of his experience with Christ. The Book of Acts records three occasions when Paul spoke about his experience of meeting Christ on the Damascus Road. Earlier he had witnessed the death of Stephen, and he had even held the coats of those who stoned Stephen. Paul had been so outraged at the Christians that he secured special papers from the high priest to go to the synagogue in Damascus to see if he could find any Christians there and put them to death. After getting the necessary papers, he began the journey from Jerusalem to Damascus, which was a trip of about 140 miles. In that day it took six days by caravan to travel that distance.

I wonder what went through Saul's mind as he was walking or riding by camel along that road. Do you suppose he asked himself, "Why would someone like Stephen die for this Christ?" or "Who was this Jesus that people were willing to die for him?"

As he approached the end of his journey, the road climbed Mount Hermon, and below lay Damascus. It is at this place that tradition says Saul was confronted by Christ. Suddenly a blinding light stopped him, and a voice like thunder addressed him. Others on the road did not see Jesus, but they heard a voice. Out of that experience, Saul became Paul. His life was transformed.

Lessons from the Damascus Road Experience

God's Initiative

We can observe certain significant facts from Jesus' meeting with Saul on the Damascus Road. One of the interesting things we discover is that it was Jesus who took the initiative in the encounter. Saul had not been searching for Jesus. In fact, he had been trying to put Jesus' disciples to death. He didn't believe in him. He thought Jesus was dead. Nevertheless, Jesus reached out and touched Saul's life.

One of the big myths of our day is that people can't come to God unless you or I "win" them to him. Now I am not saying that we shouldn't be sharing the gospel. We need to do that. But you and I will never "win" anybody to Jesus Christ. We can bear witness to Christ, but we cannot "win souls" for Christ. Salvation is God's act.

Saul's conversion underscores God's activity to reach those who seem unreachable. None of us can ever drift beyond God's care. God is always reaching out to us, even when we oppose him or turn away from him, and even when we are in the midst of sinning. The Scriptures tell us there is no place we can escape God's presence. The psalmist David asked, "Where can I go from your Spirit? Where can I flee from your presence?" (Psalms 139:7, NIV). The "Hound of Heaven" pursues us. We can truly sing: "O love that wilt not let me go." When God met Saul on the Damascus Road, God touched him and turned him around and pointed him in a new direction. Saul had become "a new creation."

Change Is Always Possible

In the story of Saul's conversion, God came into the life of another man who many thought had no possibility of changing at all. God came to Ananias in a vision and said, "Go to the street called Straight, and inquire in the house of Judas for a man of Tarsus named Saul; for behold, he is praying, and he has seen a man named Ananias come in and lay his hands on him so that he might regain his sight" (Acts 9:11–12). Ananias was terrified. He answered, "Lord, I have heard from many about this man, how much evil he has done to thy saints at Jerusalem; and here he has authority from the chief priests to bind all who call upon thy name" (vv. 13–14). Ananias could see no hope for a man like Saul. And we often have the same attitude about non-Christians. We say, "Don't waste your time with him. He's hopeless." Though we may give up on people, God does not.

A man was in conversation with a visitor to his church as they stood in the vestibule. The man said, "I can't believe all this gospel stuff. You can't really convince me that Jesus turned water into wine." "No, I probably can't convince you of that," the Christian man said. "But do you see that man standing over there? He used to be an alcoholic. Whiskey controlled his life. He was wrecking his home. He had lost his job. His whole life was in shambles. But Jesus Christ came into his life, and he was transformed. Now he has a good job and is loved by his family. I may not be able to convince you that Jesus can turn water into wine, but here is a man who was forever changed by Jesus Christ."

Jesus Christ can come into a life and bring change even in the most difficult cases. Too often we speak about Jesus Christ as though he were someone who lived only in the past and has nothing to do with the present. He is the great I Am, not the great *he was*. Jesus Christ is alive today and continues to change people's lives.

On Being Interrupted

Notice also in Saul's conversion experience that Jesus interrupted his plans. Saul had his agenda all set—he was going to Damascus to put Christians to death. When Jesus Christ came into his life, his agenda was changed. And Jesus Christ is constantly interrupting the lives of people today. We have our plans, goals, ambitions, and dreams set, and along comes Jesus Christ to slam doors shut and open new ones.

Martin Luther wanted to be a lawyer. God redirected his life, and he decided to become a monk. Then he wanted to be a teacher. God led him through all his education and preparation to be a great church reformer.

Francis of Assisi was born into great wealth. As a young man, he loved to have wild parties and engage in riotous living. One day Jesus Christ came into his life, and he cast all that aside. His father, unable to understand his son, was afraid that his son was going to give away all of his wealth. He went with his son and appealed to the bishop to stop his son from his "madness" before he gave all of his money away. He asked him to pay back what he had spent and renounce his right to his inheritance. Francis went outside the room and disrobed. He came back and stood before the bishop and his father naked with a bundle in which he had rolled his clothes and a small amount of money. These he laid before the bishop and said: "Listen, all of you and understand it well: Until this day I have called Pietro Bernadone my father, but now I desire to serve God. This is why I return him this money, for which he has given himself so much trouble, as well as my clothing, and all that I have from him, for from henceforth I desire to say nothing else than, 'Our Father, who art in heaven.'"[1] Here was a life turned around.

Albert Schweitzer, who was a noted theologian, musician, teacher, and writer, felt God tap him on the shoulder, and his life was interrupted. "Go and serve me as a medical doctor in Africa," was God's command. His life was turned in a new direction.

Tom Dooley was on assignment as a naval medical doctor in Southeast Asia during the Second World War. He had seen firsthand the desperate need there for a medical doctor. When he came back home, friends encouraged him to set up his practice as an orthopedic surgeon in the United States. But he felt God pulling him back to Southeast Asia. He went to Laos and began to practice medicine without the backing of a mission board. He felt God directing him to give his life to serve those needy people. In fact, he was the only doctor for a million people. Later he discovered that he had cancer, and he was told that he had only a short time to live. Although he was advised to stay in the United States and rest, he went back to Southeast Asia and ministered there as a doctor until death removed his hand. Why? Because God had interrupted his life and given him a new direction.

These persons, like Saul, felt God set their lives down on a new path—a path of service and ministry.

Starting Where We Are

It is important also to observe that Jesus started with Saul where he was. Sometimes we want people to live like full-grown Christians before they even come to Christ. We want them to understand all about the faith. But none of us ever understands it all. We are always in process of becoming. At the point of encounter, Saul really understood nothing. He was blind for three days until the eyes of his heart could see. Then his eyes were opened, and he went forth to serve.

I wonder what Ananias and others taught Saul during those three days. Did he listen to them tell about their experiences with Jesus Christ, his teachings, miracles, death, and resurrection? His conversion experience was only the beginning, the point of commitment. God started with him where he was, and his growth continued. Remember, conversion is not the end but the beginning of a process. Yet many never get beyond the beginning. The Christian life is to be a continuous process of becoming more like Jesus.

The First Question: "Who Are You, Lord?"

In this chapter we will address two questions from the story of Saul's conversion. The first question Saul asked was, "Who are you, Lord?" (Acts 9:5). The word "Lord" does not mean that he recognized Jesus as divine; it was simply the Jewish way of saying "sir." Thus, Saul asked, "Who are you, sir?" Jesus' response must have terrified him: "I am Jesus." Here on the road where Saul was traveling to put Christians to death, he met the Lord who had inspired these people to live and die for him. Out of this experience, which Saul had not planned or anticipated, he met Christ, and his life was forever changed.

Whenever people would talk to Paul after his conversion experience, his basic arguments were not philosophical, theological, or propositional, but based on his experience with Christ. A person might be able to disagree with some of his theological arguments, but one could not discount what he had experienced.

"Who are you, Lord?" Saul asked. "I am Jesus, whom you are persecuting" (Acts 9:5). *Now wait a minute,* Saul may have thought to himself. *I'm not persecuting you. I am persecuting your followers.* But soon Saul would learn that whenever we persecute anybody who is seeking to serve in the name of Christ, we are persecuting our Lord himself, for Jesus said, "As you did it to one of the least of these my brethren, you did it to me" (Matthew 25:40).

The anger Saul directed against the Christians was also aimed at Jesus. I wonder why Saul had so much anger toward the Christians. Was his anger partially because he thought they might be right and this Jesus could be the Messiah, and he had not yet recognized him? We are not certain why his anger was so intense, but in his anger he had persecuted the Lord himself. Tenderly and gently our Lord affirmed his close relationship to his body, the church.

The Second Question: "What Shall I Do, Lord?"

The second question we discover in Saul's conversion story is found in Acts 22. After Jesus confronted Saul, Saul asked, "What shall I do, Lord?" (v. 10, NIV). Saul learned that Christ's will was to govern his life, and he yielded in obedience. He gave up selfish ambitions that he might walk in the way of Christ.

Six times the phrase "the Way," is used in the Book of Acts. The disciples were men of the Way. Christians are followers of Christ's way. The Scriptures often make reference to God's way. "Teach me thy way, O LORD, and lead me on a level path" (Psalm 27:11). "This is the way, walk in it" (Isaiah 30:21). Jesus Christ himself declared: "I am the way, and the truth, and the life; no one comes to the Father, but by me" (John 14:6).

Paul would later use the phrase "in Christ" to refer to his relationship to Christ. Now he was not in control of his own life, but Christ was directing it, guiding it, and leading him further into his way. He had discovered a "new covenant"—a covenant not written on stone, but written in his heart. He had a new beginning of life that opened for him a vital relationship with the living God.

Acknowledge Our Sin

Look further at the question, "What shall I do, Lord?" God had addressed Paul very personally, just as he addresses you and me. Sometimes we come to Christ out of our own sense of sinfulness. We have become involved in sins that suddenly have become our Trojan horses. We thought we could handle them. But now our sin of drug or alcohol abuse or something else dominates our life. It is now in charge of us, directing us, distorting us, and ruining us. Christ comes to give us new direction and new hope out of our sinfulness. At other times our life is dominated by guilt over sins we have committed or things we have not done. We search for release from that guilt and the opportunity to begin anew.

Several years ago I came across a *Peanuts* cartoon that was published a few days after the first of the year. Lucy and Charlie Brown are engaged in conversation. "Do you know, I have decided this year I am going to set new goals for myself," Charlie Brown says. "There are things I am going to do. I'm going to accomplish something. I'm going to forget about last year and start anew. I'm really going to make new resolutions. I'm going to accomplish something this year." "I've tried that before," Lucy says. "It didn't work. What I'm going to do this year is regret. I'm going to cry over spilled milk. I'm going to cry over lost loves. I'm going to cry over broken resolutions. This is going to be my year to do nothing but regret."

A lot of us live out our lives doing nothing but regretting. Christ comes into our lives to give us forgiveness and a chance to begin anew. The Christ who could change Paul's life—a murderer—and give him another chance can come into your life and mine and change us. He gives us a new birth, a new place of beginning again.

In the Bishop's Garden at the Washington Cathedral stands a statue called *Reconciliation,* which depicts the prodigal son being received as he comes home to his father. The two are intertwined with their arms wrapped around each other, and father and son can hardly be distinguished as the father embraces his son and draws him back to himself. The statue is symbolic of God's love reaching out to sinners and reconciling them to himself.

Confront Our Need

Sometimes Christ meets us in our time of need, when we are overwhelmed with problems we don't know how to handle. Who is sufficient to carry the heavy load of losing a spouse? Who is sufficient to bear the burden of the weeks, months, or years of the suffering of a loved one who is slowly dying of cancer? Who is sufficient to bear the pain of losing a child in an accident? Who is sufficient to mend the brokenness that sometimes occurs in our lives? God moves into our lives and says, "You are not alone. I am here to sustain you."

Our needs take many shapes or forms. We may have lost a job, experienced a divorce, moved across the United States or to another country, have problems with our children. We may feel lonely and depressed, or we may long to feel loved, accepted, and affirmed by family or friends. Our needs, hopes, longings, and aspirations are as varied as we are as individuals. However, the gospel message assures us that Christ comes into our lives to love us, forgive us, comfort us, direct us, and fill our life with meaning and direction.

The presence of Christ assures us that no sorrow is too deep, no sin too severe, no difficulty so wide, no failure so final, no defeat so hard, and no problem so insurmountable that Jesus cannot give us the strength and the courage to find hope, guidance, and confidence. When our load is too heavy to bear, we draw on the strength Christ gives to us and affirm with Paul, "I can do all things in him [Christ]" (Philippians 4:13).

Recognize Our Responsibility

Look again at the question, "What shall I do, Lord?" The focus here is on doing. Christ comes into your life saying that you have responsibility. The Christian faith is not just the responsibility of your brother or sister or your pastor or other staff ministers. You are responsible for sharing the faith with others.

Sometimes we think, "I can't do much, so I won't do anything." I will never forget a man who had a great influence on me. We called him "Pop" Ottinger. For thirty years he was scoutmaster of the scout troop in the church I attended as a young man. Pop had about a sixth-grade education, and he worked as a mechanic. Week after week he volunteered his time to help boys with their efforts to reach manhood. This man, who was not even a member of my home church, uncovered the path to God for me, and I became a Christian. He was not educated, but he was dedicated. That is, he did something.

"What shall I *do*, Lord?" We are called to be doers of the Word and not hearers only. God does not want us to separate faith and works, beliefs and behavior, doctrines and deeds. A Christian's life must have a balance of both if that person is to impact society at all. We are compelled to go into the world and share God's grace with others so they too may experience his power and presence in their lives. As we share from our experience as Paul did, we should say with him, "Woe to me if I do not preach the gospel!" (1 Corinthians 9:16).

Why did David Livingstone go to Africa? Did anybody make him? He had a sense of "I must." Why did Bill Wallace go to China? "I must," he felt. Why did Bach and Beethoven write their music? Nobody forced them. They had an inner compulsion to share the Good News through music. Why did Karl Barth write dozens of books about Christ? Nobody made him. It was his way of sharing the gospel of Christ with others. He was bearing witness to the faith. Each of us needs a sense of compulsion to share the good news of Christ with others.

Several years ago in one of our national forests, a three-year-old child became lost while camping with her parents. The parents and rescue workers spent hours tramping through the forest trying to find the child. Finally, at the close of the day, they found the child sitting in a deep ravine, scratched and tired but well. The elated parents brought her back to their camp, and as the father was tucking her into her sleeping bag, she looked up at him and asked, "Daddy, aren't you glad you found me?"

God is always glad when he finds a lost person. God is the only one who can rescue lost persons and give them an opportunity to begin again. Since he has found us, we need to share our story with others so they too can have a fresh start in life. Reach out and share the love you have experienced. Helping someone begin again will bring you a sense of joy.

Note

1. Elizabeth Goudge, *My God and My All: The Life of St. Francis of Assisi* (New York: Coward-McCann, Inc., 1959), 47.

Questions for Thought and Discussion

1. Many say you can't teach an old dog new tricks. In other words, people don't change. Discuss whether or not you really believe it is possible to begin again in Christ. If so, discuss how.

2. Examine the apostle Paul's conversion experience as recorded in Acts 9:1–19; 22:5–16; 26:12–18. Discuss some lessons from that Damascus Road experience that will help your church understand Christian conversion better.

3. Ask your group to discuss whether or not we "win" anybody to Christ. What is God's initiative, and what is our own initiative and the response of the person to whom we are witnessing?

4. Discuss what it means to speak of how Christ can interrupt the lives of people and point them in new directions. Give some examples from the chapter and from your own life experience.

5. Answer Paul's question to Christ on the Damascus Road as though it were addressed to you personally: "What shall I do, Lord?" Allow time for each member of your group to respond.

CHAPTER 9

Christians
Unashamed

EVERY ONE OF US MUST CONFESS THAT WE SOMETIMES FEEL a sense of shame. There are things in my past that I would not want projected on a screen for others to see, and I'm sure you feel the same. There are also times when I'm ashamed of things I see other people doing. One glance at a newspaper will reveal a variety of shameful acts—robberies, murders, rapes, and white-collar corruption. We all feel a sense of shame that people commit such crimes.

The apostle Paul was no stranger to shame. He wrote about his personal sense of shame in persecuting the early Christians. He also wrote that he was ashamed of Christians who fought among themselves and engaged in immorality, jealously, envy, self-centeredness, and strife.

But there was one thing about which the apostle Paul never had a sense of shame: He was "not ashamed" of the gospel of Jesus Christ. He wrote in Romans 1:16, "I am not ashamed of the gospel: it is the power of God for salvation to every one who has faith, to the Jew first and also to the Greek." Evidently, some early followers of Christ were

112

ashamed, or Paul would not have had to make that pronouncement. He wanted to make his position clear.

Have you ever wondered why some of the early Christians may have felt a sense of shame? I think there were several reasons. For one thing, Christianity seemed so insignificant. You and I are familiar with the impact of Christianity over the past two thousand years, but when the early Christians looked around, they saw that the church was composed mostly of the outcasts of society. Few significant leaders of society were a part of the early Christian church. Thus, the early Christians felt powerless when they looked at the well-educated Greeks and the wealth, power, and prestige of Rome. What could a relatively small group of Christians do against all the great power of Rome and Greece? Yet the Christian gospel withstood all the power of Rome, and Christianity marched on even after the fall of Rome.

First-century Christians were often the subject of ridicule and disparagement, because the gospel was "foolishness" to many. When Christians would gather for communion services, Jews would report all kinds of tales about what they were doing. They were accused of drinking blood and eating human flesh, and many thought they were cannibals. They were also accused of engaging in immoral behavior because men and women met together for the so-called love feasts behind closed doors. Because Christians would not bow down to the statue of the emperor in the center of the city plaza, they were accused of being unpatriotic and guilty of treason. The gospel seemed too radical and was a stumbling block to the Jews. Thus, being a Christian in that day was difficult.

An ancient painting on a stone wall was unearthed a number of years ago that reveals the unpopularity of the early Christians. The painting depicted Christ hanging on a cross, and instead of the head of Jesus, they had in its place the head of a donkey—an ass. Underneath were written these words: "Alex the Jew worships his god." This was the kind of disdain and ridicule that was often directed against the early Christians. Because it was so unpopular to be a Christian, many hung their heads in shame or would not admit that they were Christians at all.

But not the apostle Paul. Moffat and Barclay have translated the familiar Romans 1:16 in the positive phrasing, "I am proud of the gospel of Jesus Christ." Paul was not ashamed of the gospel; he was proud of it! He was willing to suffer for the gospel. He had been imprisoned, stoned, beaten, ridiculed, run out of towns, and rejected in many ways.

Paul had longed to share the gospel with Rome, and in his letter to that church, he was writing to a people he didn't know and to a church he had never visited. Knowing that his epistle might be one of the few pieces of Christian literature they had ever seen, he wanted to challenge them to deeper commitment by affirming his own strong faith. So, Paul set forth his own credentials as an apostle of Christ and sounded a trumpet call to the believers in Rome, exhorting them to understand and experience the grace of God through Christ, a gospel that he hoped to share with them personally one day.

Today many are either embarrassed or too timid to speak boldly about Jesus. Paul's boldness is a model for us in proclaiming the message that God was in Christ reconciling the world unto himself.

The Gospel

Paul declared in Romans 1:16 that he was not ashamed of "the gospel." What is the gospel? A young boy playing the part of a Christmas angel in a church play can instruct us. His line was, "Behold, I bring you good tidings of great joy!" For days he would come down to the breakfast table with those words on his lips. And when he bounded in the door after school, he would repeat them. Then came the night of the play. When it was time to say his line, he went blank. He hesitated for a moment and then moved over to the edge of the stage and exclaimed, "Say, have I got news for you!" Indeed, we do have news about God—great news! That is the gospel.

You and I live in an age in which we dare not be ashamed of the good news that God has revealed himself to us in Jesus Christ. In Jesus we see what God is like. People ask again and again, on college campuses, on street corners, in stores, in homes, at work, and in all places in society, "What is God like?" We must point them to Jesus Christ and what the Gospels tell us about him. From Jesus' life we can get an understanding of God's nature and being.

Why do people look for another sign of God's existence? What sign would they accept today as greater evidence than the sign we have already had in Jesus Christ? Suppose while we were sitting in church, a hand would suddenly begin to write across the wall: "I am alive; I really exist," signed God. Would people believe more in the existence of God because of that? Or would they assume someone was playing a hoax? What other sign do we need? God has revealed himself to us in Jesus Christ. Is that not sign enough!

A number of years ago one of the most famous twentieth-century theologians, Karl Barth, came to the United States and lectured at a number of prominent universities and seminaries. When he finished speaking at the University of Chicago and had a time of dialogue with students, one of the students raised his hand and said: "Dr. Barth, I would like to ask you one question. If you could summarize the gospel in one sentence, what would you say?" Remember that Barth was a theologian noted for his complex scholarly books. He never stated anything simply but at great length. Barth puffed on his pipe for a moment and then replied, "Jesus loves me this I know, for the Bible tells me so."

The Scriptures tell us the good news of what God has done in Jesus Christ. In him we have seen the love of God and have been offered salvation and life. That is good news, and I am not ashamed of that. It resounds within my being, and I am proud to tell others about God's great love. You and I should live daily with a sense of great pride in the gospel.

The Power of God

I am not ashamed of the gospel, because it is "the power of God." We know something about power in our age. When we jump into our cars and turn the key, power will suddenly come to life under the hood. If the engine fails, we face frustration and difficulties. And we have all seen awesome power in the natural world—earthquakes, volcanoes, tornadoes, hurricanes, and lightning. We are also familiar with monetary power, military power, political power, and other kinds of power. But the power Paul is speaking of in Romans 1:16 is the supernatural power of the Holy Spirit within us that motivates us and gives us the ability to reach beyond our natural, fleshly limitations.

We have all seen the awesome power of the natural world. We have seen the devastation of hurricanes and tornadoes, of ice storms and flood waters. In Switzerland, I gazed at the mountains formed by the power of ancient glaciers. I have stood at Niagara Falls and watched tons of water pour over that cliff. I have traveled out West and seen the earth split asunder by an earthquake. In Hawaii I saw the glowing trails of lava that had been spewed from the bowels of a volcano and spilled over the earth's surface—lava so molten that months later its coals were still red hot.

You and I have witnessed something, too, of the power of humankind. We are familiar with monetary power, military power, nuclear power, political power, and Black Power. But there is also a power called motivation. This power stimulates you and me to reach beyond ourselves, beyond what we know and have experienced. It is exercised in various ways; each person is motivated by different things and in different degrees—by parents or teachers, by music or literature, by history or by a vision of the future. Motivation comes in diverse and unexpected ways.

When I was a young boy, my friends and I used to go swimming in Dr. Pew's lake. Dr. Pew worked in town as a medical doctor and had a farm on the edge of my hometown. In order to get to the lake, we would have to ride our bicycles five miles into the country, leave them under a bridge, and hike a mile through a cow pasture. Well, we had finished the ride and hike one day, and after swimming all afternoon, we were tired. We didn't think we would have enough energy to walk through that cow pasture to get to the other side. In fact, we could hardly lift up one foot after another as we crossed it. Suddenly, from the corner of my eye, I saw Dr. Pew's bull coming toward us. It was amazing how suddenly life came into our tired legs and how quickly we moved across that field and jumped the fence to safety. What had happened? We had experienced the power of motivation that came to us from an external force—the bull.

Sooner or later all of us discover various kinds of motivating powers that come to us from many sources. Today beliefs and ideas provide motivation for much of our action, but the ancient Romans did not trust the power of ideas. Their strength came from the power of weapons and oppression, which they used to move their empire across the world. The spread of Christianity, however, was empowered by the Holy Spirit moving within and motivating individuals. Christianity's message was that the greatest power in the world was God's love. To many of the ancient people, the power of God had been a terrifying thing. They believed God was to be feared and avoided. The gospel message proclaimed that God was not to be dreaded but was loving and to be loved.

Jesus did not come into the world to use power in a devastating way to force people to love God. He will not browbeat us or manipulate us into loving God. Instead, he will love us into following God. Jesus said: "I, when I am lifted up from the earth, will draw all men to myself" (John 12:32). God reaches into the lives of all who will open them to demonstrate the awesome power of divine love.

God's power came in the form of a servant. Philippians 2:7–8 says that Jesus "emptied himself, taking the form of a servant, . . . and humbled himself and became obedient unto death, even death on a cross." Jesus' love was not the power of force and might but of sacrificial love. This power was not limited to the first century but continues today to make us radically different as we open our lives to God's presence.

Power of God for Salvation

Paul said, "I am not ashamed of the gospel, because it is the power of God for the salvation of everyone who believes" (Romans 1:16, NIV). Do you know that you and I belong to the only organization, the church, that gathers together every week and begins its meeting with the acknowledgment that we are gathered together as sinners? We are sinners saved by grace. We are aware that we need something beyond ourselves to bring us into right relationship with God, and God's grace comes to us while we are still sinners.

We do not like to talk about sin. One of my favorite philosophers, Charles Schultz, the writer of *Peanuts*, makes the point in one of his comic strips. Lucy is talking to Charlie Brown, and she says something to him that a lot of us may have difficulty with: "The whole trouble with you, Charlie Brown, is that you will not listen to the whole trouble with you." The whole trouble with all of us is that we will not listen to the whole trouble with us.

The Scriptures ring with the affirmation that "all have sinned and fall short of the glory of God" (Romans 3:23). They attest to the reality that sin has cut us off from our own self, others, and most importantly, God. Salvation is God's gift to you and to me, and out of the awareness that we are sinners grows our sense of the need of God's redemption. Sin brings shame. Some feel defeated by the awareness of sin's costs and scars. But the gospel is the good news that God's grace has broken into our world in Jesus Christ not to condemn us but to love us and redeem us.

A number of years ago Dr. Eugene Laubach, a minister in New York City, took his young son to see the movie *Tom Sawyer*. While they were watching the movie, his son suddenly began to cry. Dr. Laubach leaned over to his son and asked, "Son, what's wrong?" In the movie, at this particular moment, Tom had slipped into the house of Aunt Polly, the woman who had raised him, at night and had put a token under her pillow so that she would know he had been there. He leaned over and kissed her on the cheek and then climbed out the window and ran away. The lad looked up at his father and said, "Daddy, Tom loves her, but she doesn't know it."

The good news is that God loves you and me, and we ought to know it. In fact, "God so loved the world that he gave his only begotten Son." That is something about which you and I need never feel a sense of shame. God has loved us, and in Jesus Christ we have moved from death to life, enslavement to freedom. The Lord has given us new birth, a new beginning. I am not ashamed of that.

A Gift for Everyone

Paul concludes Romans 1:16 with, "to every one who has faith, to the Jew first and also to the Greek." Faith is the foundation of our belief. We make a commitment of absolute trust to the God who has revealed himself in Christ Jesus. Faith is an acknowledgment of our total reliance on God and not on any works that come from our human efforts. As the old hymn says, "Nothing in my hand I bring; simply to thy cross I cling." Salvation by faith alone, Paul declared, is available to everyone. It is not just for the wealthy, the powerful, or the famous. And it is not just for me and you. It is for all who will open their lives to receive God's love.

The gospel tells us of the awesome love that God has for individuals. We live in an age in which individuals often get lost and forgotten. But God works through the faith of individuals. We forget that it was Noah who by faith obeyed all that God commanded and saved the human race by building an ark; it was Moses who stood before Pharaoh and was used to deliver God's people Israel; and later it was Joseph in Pharaoh's court who saved Israel during a great famine. Think of the difference David's leadership made for Israel. Look at how the disciples impacted the world in their day and how Paul took the gospel to the Gentile world in his day. We could go on down through the centuries noting how one individual here and there made a tremendous difference in other places.

We sometimes think that individuals do not count, but they have made all the difference down through the ages. Did you know, for example, that the decision to behead Charles I was made by one vote; that Thomas Jefferson was elected president by one vote; that the construction of the Erie Canal was authorized by one vote; that the states of Texas, Oregon, and California came into the Union by one vote? Individuals have made a great deal of difference.

On the occasion of receiving an honorary doctor of humanities degree from the University of Louisville, the late Samuel D. Proctor, pastor of Abyssinian Baptist Church in New York City and professor emeritus at Rutgers University, noted in his graduation address the difference one person can make when he told about his grandmother who was born a slave and emancipated without a single possession or family. Nevertheless, she later attended and graduated from a small black college that was founded by a religious denomination after the Civil War. Two generations later there are seventy-two college graduates, including nineteen with doctorates, who are direct descendants of this one woman. "That's one of the quietest revolutions you ever heard in your life," Proctor said. "She did it without an aristocracy of blood or money. There is no aristocracy at all like the aristocracy of the mind and the spirit."[1]

Individuals who have committed their lives to Christ and work in their community can make all the difference in influencing it for Jesus Christ. The power of evil is great, but I have made a vow that I will not let the power of evil keep me from doing what I can do in God's kingdom to combat it. You too can make a real difference.

In churches I have pastored, I have known young people and adults who have made all the difference in their communities because of their committed lives. I can see the face of one woman who has touched the lives of hundreds of young people through her committed work in music. I see a tall man who taught a Sunday school class of junior boys for forty years. Now these boys are grown and married, but they still talk about this man and the impact he made on their lives. Other faces rush before me and, I'm sure, before you. You and I can make a difference where we are. You and I are individuals who have experienced salvation and have felt the power of God, and we should never be ashamed of it.

Do not live in this world with your head hanging down. Enter into life with a new sense of meaning and enthusiasm. Let your flag of faith wave proudly when the winds of change come. Continue your journey with a new song in your heart and a new spring in your step. Live your life as an affirmation of Paul's words: "I am not ashamed of the gospel: it is the power of God for salvation to everyone who has faith."

Note

1. *The Courier Journal* (Louisville, Ky.), May 22, 1989.

Questions for Thought and Discussion

1. Discuss why you think some believers in the first century might have been ashamed of being Christians. Do you think this attitude is still a problem for the church today? Why or why not?

2. What did the apostle Paul mean when he declared, "I am *not ashamed* of the gospel of Jesus Christ"(Romans 1:16)?

3. Define the word *gospel*.

4. Discuss Paul's phrase in Romans 1:16, "power of God for salvation." Define the meaning of *power* as demonstrated in the ministry of Jesus, and talk about what *salvation* means today.

5. Ask various persons in your group to share a time when they were ashamed or embarrassed to witness for Christ. What caused that response? What can be done to overcome that attitude?

6. Share some reasons a Christian may have a sense of enthusiasm and boldness in witnessing for Christ.

The *Church*
AS AN
EVANGELISTIC
Community

BRUCE LARSON, PASTOR OF THE UNIVERSITY PRESBYTERIAN
Church in Seattle, Washington, recalled an experience
he had when he was a student at Princeton Divinity School.
Some zealous seminary students decided they wanted to
evangelize Princeton University. They collected thousands of
empty medicine bottles and stuffed them with Scripture
verses. Then they walked through the dorms at Princeton
University and tossed the bottles into students' rooms. The
president of the university was very upset by this action and
called Dr. MacKay, the seminary president, to protest this
action. The next morning in chapel, Dr. MacKay, who had
served as a noted missionary for many years, was close to
tears as he rebuked the students. "I don't question your zeal,
but you have set back the cause of Christ in this place. It is
my sincere desire that our seminary might be an influence
on this great university. If you want to reach those students,
go over there and make friends with them. Don't dash in and
out with a bunch of tricks."[1]

Too often the church has tried to do evangelism with gimmicks and gadgets. Effective evangelism is not accomplished

in an instant. The church cannot rely on a flash-in-the-pan mass appeal to reach large groups for Christ and cause them to come rushing into the church. The church needs to guard itself against looking for magic methods of evangelism, because the most effective evangelism down through the centuries has been done one on one.

Christianity is always one generation away from extinction. If you and I do not share the message of Christ with others, the church will cease to exist. One person tells another about Christ, and he or she tells another, and so on. The task of evangelism is never complete. The church's message has to be shared again and again with each new generation.

As persons are brought to Christ, they are also called to identify with his church, for whom he laid down his life. Jesus said, "I will build my church, and the gates of Hades will not overcome it" (Matthew 16:18, NIV). New Christians need to identify with the church in order to grow and be nurtured in the faith. The New Testament is clear that the church is Christ's instrument for reaching people with his love and is the community where Christians develop and grow in the faith.

One of the most powerful epistles in the New Testament about the significance of the church is Paul's Letter to the Ephesians, written by Paul while a prisoner in Rome. Among other things, he addresses the importance and function of the church as well as its organization and administration.

Gifts for Ministry

In Ephesians 4:11–16 Paul uses three themes to address the church as an evangelistic community. Paul begins by saying that God's gifts "prepare God's people for works of service" (v. 12). Paul refers to some of these gifts, though not all. Some were apostles, a limited number who were witnesses to the resurrection. The prophets, next in Paul's list, were "forthtellers." They were not predicting future events, but were pronouncing the judgment of God on persons who were disobedient to God. The evangelists mentioned here were missionaries who traveled from one city to another witnessing for Christ. Pastor-teachers were the ones who taught the church the doctrines of the Christian way. Paul gives a much longer list of gifts in 1 Corinthians 12:28–30.

In 1 Corinthians 12:11 Paul notes, "All these are the work of one and the same Spirit, and he gives them to each one, just as he determines." Thus, all persons have been gifted by God for service. Roman Catholic theologian Ronald Knox has observed that "the church in heaven is all saints, but the church on earth is all sorts." From the bell-ringer to the theologian, each person is important in the work of ministry.

Equipped for Ministry

The first purpose of spiritual gifts is that the church be "prepared" (NIV) for ministry in the world. The word for *prepare* in Greek is used of setting a broken bone, mending a fisherman's nets, and bringing opposing sides together in political circles. It represents a means of putting a thing or person in right condition. To equip or prepare something or someone is to enable that thing or person to fulfill its rightful purpose.

The church is equipped for the purpose of carrying on the ministry of Christ. The church is the base for training members and launching Christ's ministry into the world. We misunderstand the purpose of the church if we think the church is an end in itself. In its buildings the church is trained to scatter into the world to serve its Lord.

Cultivating the Spiritual Quality of the Church

If the church is to be an evangelistic community, it must have the spiritual quality of its Lord. If the church is not different from the world, non-Christians will ask, "Why should I be a part of something that is no different from where I am now?" Carl E. Braaten, a noted contemporary theologian, wrote: "The worst form of success that we could have as a congregation is this: We could get lots of new members, all transferring from the world into the church without any basic change in themselves. What will happen is that not being changed themselves, they will surely change the church, remaking it into a pagan shrine."[2] In other words, they will bring the world's standards into the church, and soon the church will be remade in the image of the world. Our mission is not to bring the world into the church but to take the gospel into the world.

A woman was walking with a tour group through Westminster Abbey one day. The tour guide pointed out the tombs of famous persons who were buried there and noted the grandeur of that great old English cathedral. But this little old lady was unimpressed. Finally she said to the guide, "Young man, stop all of your chatter. I want to ask you a question. Has anybody been saved here lately?"

That is a significant question for every church. Has anybody met Christ through your church's ministry lately? The church was not created to be a museum or showplace. It was founded to lead persons to commitment to Christ and his way.

Bearing Witness for Christ

If the church is truly equipped for ministry, it will be witnessing for Christ. The last words of our Lord recorded by Matthew were the Great Commission: "Go therefore and make disciples of all nations" (Matthew 28:19). In the Book of Acts, Luke gives us the last words of Jesus to his disciples before he departed: "You shall be my witnesses in Jerusalem and in all Judea and Samaria and to the end of the earth" (Acts 1:8). The church was commissioned by the Lord to bear witness, so it must equip people to share the good news of Christ. If the church is not bearing witness for our Lord, then surely we are not fulfilling the purpose for which Christ established the church.

Gabriel Marcel has said, "I am obliged to bear witness, because I hold as if it were, a particle of light, and to keep it to myself would be equivalent to extinguishing it." You and I have the light of God's love in our lives, and if we do not share it, we extinguish it. Christians are to be light, salt, and leaven in the world to influence it for Christ. A true witness has to speak. To remain silent is not to be a witness.

New Testament scholar Stephen Neill has reminded the church of its calling to witness.

> It is not permitted for a minister to say I am not an evangelist . . . The minister is ordained for the purpose of bringing men and women to Christ; if he is not doing it, it is questionable whether he ought to be in the ministry at all. Equally, it is not open for a layman to say, "I cannot be an evangelist." If he is a Christian he must be a witness. If he is not willing to be a witness, it is time he gave up calling himself a Christian.[3]

The church is called to bear witness for Christ. If you and I have felt the impact of Christ's love, then we will identify ourselves with the community of that love and seek to share that Good News with others. The local church can be effective in evangelism only if a core group of members commits to becoming trained and active in the evangelistic work. That core group, ideally numbering seventy, will be symbolic of the seventy disciples whom Jesus sent out to witness. It will be their responsibility to train, challenge, equip, and direct the evangelistic efforts of the local church. I recommend that a church also establish several smaller evangelistic groups, which might be called the Society of Andrew or Fishers for People. These smaller groups would be commissioned with one-on-one evangelistic work. Hopefully, out of these groups will emerge persons willing and able to train and equip others in the ministry.

A man told his pastor one day, "I have been a member of this church for ten years. Let me tell you how I became a Christian. One day, while I was walking down Main Street, one of the members of this church, who is now deceased, stopped me and said: 'Bob, your father was a great Christian man. I think it is time you took a stand for Christ and for his church.' I thought about what he said all day long. I talked to my wife about it that night, and the next Sunday she and I made a profession of faith. Since that moment, I have been a faithful member of this church. I am convinced that the reason our church has baptized only nine persons in the last ten years is because no one has bothered to invite another person to come to Christ. I want to challenge our church to change that."

The church is charged with the weighty task of equipping persons to witness for Christ in the world. As members of the body of Christ, we ought to be burdened that others do not know the joy of his forgiving love. Let us pray and equip ourselves to serve him well.

Building Up the Church

Second, Paul said, the purpose of the church is to build up the body of Christ. The purpose of all Christians is to be *constructive* not *de*structive. We are to be a part of the solution not a part of the problem. And in order to build up the body, we need to be building specific areas of our faith and service.

Building Unity

The purpose of our gifts, Paul notes, is to bring about the unity of the faith. Unity is a sign of the maturity of a church. The church recognizes diversity within this unity because of the variety of gifts possessed by its members. Disunity is a sign of an immature church. Strife, quarrels, divisions, and dissension are signs of the immaturity of the people in a congregation, and any witness for Christ is ruined.

William Willimon, minister at Duke University, shared an experience he had with a man he was trying to get to join his church when he was a pastor. This man had visited his church for several Sundays, had attended a Sunday school class, and had even come to the Wednesday night supper. Several weeks passed by, and Dr. Willimon telephoned the man to see if he had made up his mind about joining the church. "In the beginning I really liked your church," the man said. "I liked the worship services, and I enjoyed visiting in the church classes. But frankly—I don't really mean this as criticism—but the better I got to know your people, the more I disliked them."[4]

What was the man saying? When persons visit a church and find it filled with strife, quarrels, dissension, and negativism, they simply do not want to be a part of that. That is what the world is like. They don't want to be part of a congregation that is torn apart by the same struggles they see in the world. The English theologian William Temple put his finger on this problem when he observed: "If the man who observes from outside sees no Christian graces in those who are inside, if congregations are quarrelsome or self-complacent, then no amount of preaching can counteract the harm that is done. The presupposition of effective evangelism and the first step toward achieving it, is a truly dedicated church."[5] We will never be an effective witness for Christ unless we have a spirit of unity, togetherness, graciousness, love, and concern for one another. We can build up the body of Christ by loving, caring, supporting, and seeking to find the best in others as we witness for Christ.

Christ is our unity—not creeds, doctrines, or styles of worship. With Christ as our unity and model, we can reach outside the church to all kinds of persons, as he did when he was on earth.

Building Stewardship

Another way we build up the church is through faithful stewardship. We have to undergird evangelism with our financial support. We can't assume that somebody else is going to shoulder the cost of sharing the good news. Each

Christian has a responsibility to share his or her financial gifts as well as other gifts. A man complained to another member of his church one Sunday during their stewardship drive, "It's expensive to belong to this church." And the other member responded, "It should be, because it cost our Lord his life!" Having received so much through Christ's church because of this costly love, we should be eager to support the church.

Building Pastoral Care

Pastoral care, by both the pastoral staff and by laypersons in the congregation, is a necessity if we expect to build up the church. If persons feel their church does not care for their needs, they will not want to be a part of that congregation. The congregation I serve has many pastoral care ministries. The Job Club, the counseling center, the Alzheimer's Day Care Center, the kindergarten, the Mother's Day Out, the miscellaneous support groups, and other pastoral care programs all are ways of saying, "We care about you and your needs." Caring for persons in their time of illness or grief or in other times of crises is our church's way of showing Christ's love and support to them. Pastoral care is our church's way of saying that we are concerned about the total person. And all that we do, we do in the name of Jesus Christ. Pastoral care is our cup of cold water for the thirsty, clothing for those who are naked, and bread for the hungry. We attempt to show care as a congregation whenever and wherever we are aware of a human need. And we seek to meet that need in the name of Christ.

A woman came to see the pastor of a church near where she lived. She shared with him a heavy burden she had just discovered. She had been married to a man for fourteen years, and they had two children. But now she had learned that her husband was getting ready to run off with his secretary. She didn't know what to do, so she came to ask advice of this neighborhood pastor. The minister told her that he wasn't sure what she should do either, but he would think and pray about it and let her know. He decided to ask different couples in his congregation to make a friendly visit to their home. He did not explain why.

On Monday night a couple from the church visited the woman and her husband and expressed friendliness and concern for their children. Others visited throughout the week and showed sincere friendship. By Saturday this man came to his senses and confessed to his wife what he had planned to do but said that he was now going to break off that relationship. He begged for her forgiveness. After she forgave him, he asked her to go with him to the church of her choice. She suggested, of course, that they go to the church where their visitors attended. The next day they went to church and committed their lives to Christ because the people in that congregation had expressed genuine care for them.[6] We build up the body of Christ through our loving pastoral and congregational care.

Growth toward a Mature Faith

Finally, Paul stresses that not only are we to equip the church for the work of ministry and build it up, but we are to grow into a mature faith. Paul uses two metaphors to indicate Christian immaturity (see Ephesians 4:14). Some Christians are like infants. They are gullible, caught up by every fad, and are at the mercy of every new craze that comes along. They are easily led astray. Others in their immaturity are like a rudderless boat that is tossed about by the waves of the sea. Carried by the currents of society, they move about without direction or purpose. Every false, new, or novel doctrine pulls these immature persons into its current. Christ's way is soon forsaken for the ways of the world. Paul challenges such Christians to reach for maturity in the faith.

Erik Routley, minister of the Augustine-Bristo Congregational Church in Edinburgh, Scotland, has warned the church about one of the contemporary threats to the spiritual growth of the church today in his book *Church Music and Theology.*

There is always a pressure on the church to try to be greater than its Lord. Certain forms of evangelism are tainted with this defect. It means that along with an unregenerate desire for power goes an unwillingness to encounter any tension or difficulty. There is a danger that in the composition and practice of church music the church will always turn to what is easy and familiar, seeking to bring men to Christ by a route which by-passes the way of the cross. Music which is come by in that frame of mind will not be of profit to the people of God.[7]

The church always needs to remind its members that it is committed to the way of the cross. We do not call people to a cult of the familiar or easy way, or to paths of positive or possibility thinking, or to what is cute and sweet. The church calls persons to take up their cross and follow Christ.

Called to Be Disciples

If we are going to be mature in our faith, we have to realize that we are called to be disciples. The word *disciple* means "learner." Disciples are always seeking to learn more about Christ and his way. No Christian can ever say that he or she has learned all there is to know about Christ. We are lifetime learners—always seeking to know more about our faith. And Christian growth does not happen automatically. The seed that has been sown in our heart by faith has to be cultivated.

No person has given his or her life totally to Christ. We always have areas in our life in which we need to be converted. We need constantly to be praying, "Not my will but thine be done," because we harbor some secret chamber that we do not want to give to Christ. The spiritual battle is never finally won; it is a lifetime struggle. To grow and mature into Christ's image, we have to be open to God's leadership. Herman Melville wrote, "I love all men who dive. Any fish can swim near the surface, but it takes a great whale to go downstairs five miles or more." As Christians, we need to probe deeply into our faith so we can grow strong. Surface knowledge should never be enough for us.

Another way we mature in our faith is by drawing upon our fellow Christians for strength and guidance. We need the gifts of others to make our spiritual life complete. E. Y. Mullins related in his small book *Talks on Soul Winning* a story about a ten-year-old boy who made a profession of faith in his church. After the boy had been received by the church and had been given the hand of fellowship, an old man with gray hair and a gray beard walked up to him and took his hand and said: "My little brother, you are the youngest member of this church, and I am the oldest. I need you because you are young and have life and enthusiasm, and you need me because I am older and have wisdom and can help to advise and guide you. Let us promise each other to be brothers and lend each other a helping hand."[8]

We need one another in the church. Stephen Boyd, basing his research on sixteenth-century Anabaptist Pilgram Marpeck, has called this sharing in the body of Christ "the sacramental community." Marpeck believed that the community in all its concrete particulars is where the reality of Christ is experienced.[9] This was our Lord's vision of the church and the dream Paul wrote about in Ephesians.

Called to Spiritual Growth

The minimum requirements for Christian spiritual growth are (1) daily prayer and Bible reading, (2) regular weekly worship, (3) small group participation, (4) faithful stewardship, and (5) Christian service. These are the least we all need to be doing if we are going to mature in our faith. If these disciplines are not a part of our life on a continuous basis, we need not question why we are not maturing in our faith. As Paul wrote young Timothy, we need to be trained in godliness (1 Timothy 4:7).

Paul says that our goal is to be like Christ, our model. Yet none of us can say that he or she has ever reached that goal. We are all still in process of trying to be like him. Paul, writing in Galatians 5:19–21, lists the characteristics of the lower nature. Then in verse 22 he declares, "But the fruit of the Spirit is love, joy, peace, patience, kindness, goodness, faithfulness, gentleness, self-control." In Colossians 3:12–14 he gives us another list of the qualities of the Christian life. "Put on then, as God's chosen ones, holy and beloved, compassion, kindness, lowliness, meekness, and patience, forbearing one another and, if one has a complaint against another, forgiving each other; . . . And above all these put on love, which binds everything together in perfect harmony."

How many of us can say that these are truly qualities that describe our lives? We know we fall far short of these standards. Jesus said, "Be perfect, therefore, as your heavenly Father is perfect" (Matthew 5:48). None of us has reached that goal. We are modeling our lives after Christ, but we never arrive. Nevertheless, we press on toward our goal.

The famous artist Doré had a student approach him one day with a painting he had done of Jesus. He wanted the master to give him his criticism of his work. The famous painter looked at it for a moment and didn't say anything. Then the young student pressed the artist for an answer. "You don't love Jesus," Doré replied, "or you would paint him better."

If you and I really love Jesus, we will always be seeking to paint him better. We will desire to be equipped for the work of ministry, to build his church, and to become mature in our faith so that we are more like him. The church, when it is truly an evangelistic community, will have all these elements as a part of its life.

Notes

1. Bruce Larson, *Wind and Fire* (Waco, Tex.: Word, 1984), 133.

2. Carl E. Braaten, *The Whole Counsel of God* (Philadelphia: Fortress, 1974), 73.

3. Charles B. Templeton, *Evangelism for Tomorrow* (New York: Harper & Row, 1957), 48.

4. William H. Willimon, *What's Right with the Church?* (San Francisco: Harper & Row, 1985), 8.

5. William Temple, *The Hope of a New World* (New York: Macmillan, 1943), 105.

6. Andrew W. Blackwood, *Evangelism in the Home Church* (New York: Abingdon-Cokesbury, 1952), 111–12.

7. Erik Routley, *Church Music and Theology* (Philadelphia: Muhlenberg Press, 1959), 56.

8. E. Y. Mullins, *Talks on Soul Winning* (Nashville: Sunday School Board of the SBC, 1920), 62–63.

9. Stephen B. Boyd, *Pilgram Marpeck: His Life and Social Theology* (Durham, N.C.: Duke University Press, 1992), 69–75, 90–96.

Questions for Thought and Discussion

1. Evangelism in some churches has meant gimmicks, cold visits to homes, one-night rallies, and immediate responses from those hearing the gospel message for the first time. How do you evaluate the effectiveness of such methods today? Give time for each person to respond.

2. Discuss what it means "to prepare God's people for works of service, so that the body of Christ may be built up." Define the word *prepare* and discuss how the church can effectively train people for ministry in today's world.

3. Define the church's mission as we have received it from our Lord. How do you think your church is measuring up to Christ's commission to go into all the world and make disciples (Matthew 28:19)?

4. Read again Gabriel Marcel's quote, "I am obliged to bear witness. . . ," and ask various persons in your group to

define the meaning of witness and its role for the contemporary church.

5. Ask for reactions to William Willimon's story relating to a man who visited his church and shared his negative feelings concerning his visits. What are the implications for your church from this story?

6. List some congregational or pastoral ministries your church is already engaged in that build bridges for communication to persons needing the love of Christ. What are some new ministries in which you might engage that will not only meet human needs but open doors for evangelism and making disciples?

7. Discuss the meaning of the word *disciple*. How do church members continue to learn and grow in the knowledge of and in their service for Christ?

8. The writer has listed five minimum requirements for spiritual growth. Do you agree with this list? Would you add others or subtract some? Give your reasons for your own list.

A SELECTED
BIBLIOGRAPHY

Adams, James R. *So You Can't Stand Evangelism*. Cambridge: Cowley, 1994.

Armstrong, James. *From the Underside: Evangelism from a Third World Vantage Point*. Maryknoll, N.Y.: Orbis, 1981.

Armstrong, Richard Stoll. *The Pastor as Evangelist*. Louisville: Westminster/John Knox, 1984.

———. *The Pastor as Evangelist in the Parish*. Louisville: Westminster/John Knox, 1990.

———. *Service Evangelism*. Philadelphia: Westminster, 1979.

Autry, C. E. *The Theology of Evangelism*. Nashville: Broadman, 1966.

Barclay, William. *Fishers of Men*. Philadelphia: Westminster, 1966.

Borchet, Gerald L. *Dynamics of Evangelism*. Waco: Word, 1976.

Brueggemann, Walter. *Biblical Perspective and Evangelism*. Nashville: Abingdon, 1993.

Campolo, Tony. *Following Jesus without Embarrassing God*. Dallas: Word, 1997.

Chafin, Kenneth L. *The Reluctant Witness.* Nashville: Broadman, 1974.

Coalten, Milton J., and Virgil Cruz, editors. *How Shall We Witness?* Louisville: Westminster/ John Knox, 1995.

Coleman, Robert E. *Evangelism on the Cutting Edge.* Old Tappan, N.J.: Revell, 1986.

———. *The Master Plan of Discipleship.* Old Tappan, N.J.: Revell, 1987.

———. *The Master Plan of Evangelism.* Old Tappan, N.J.: Revell, 1972.

Conn, Walter E. *Christian Conversion: A Developmental Interpretation of Autonomy and Surrender.* New York: Paulist Press, 1986.

Dale, Robert D., and Delos Miles. *Evangelizing the Hard-to-Reach.* Nashville: Broadman, 1984.

DeWire, Harry A. *The Christian as Communicator.* Philadelphia: Westminster, 1961.

Doohan, Leonard. *Laity's Mission in the Local Church.* San Francisco: Harper & Row, 1986.

Edge, Findley B. *The Greening of the Church.* Waco, Tex.: Word, 1971.

Ford, Leighton. *The Christian Persuader.* New York: Harper & Row, 1966.

Franke, Gabriel. *Word in Deed: The Theological Themes in Evangelism.* Grand Rapids: Eerdmans, 1975.

Gibbs, Eddie. *The God Who Communicates: A Call to Effective Communication in Evangelism.* London: Hodder and Stoughton, 1985.

Gilkey, Langdon. *How the Church Can Minister to the World without Losing Itself.* New York: Harper & Row, 1964.

Green, Bryan. *The Practice of Evangelism.* New York: Scribners, 1951.

Green, Michael. *Evangelism in the Early Church.* Grand Rapids: Eerdmans, 1970.

Hale, J. Russell. *The Unchurched: Who They Are and Why They Stay Away.* San Francisco: Harper & Row, 1980.

Hartt, Julian N. *Toward a Theology of Evangelism.* New York: Abingdon, 1955.

Henderson, Robert T. *Joy to the World: An Introduction to Kingdom Evangelism.* Atlanta: John Knox, 1980.

Hendrick, John R. *Opening the Door of Faith.* Atlanta: John Knox, 1977.

Hinson, William H. *A Place to Dig In: Doing Evangelism in the Local Church.* Nashville: Abingdon, 1987.

Holmes, Urban T. *Turning to Christ: A Theology of Renewal and Evangelization.* New York: Seabury, 1981.

Hunter, George G. *The Contagious Congregation: Frontiers in Evangelism and Church Growth.* Nashville: Abingdon, 1979.

Johnson, Ben. *An Evangelism Primer.* Atlanta: John Knox, 1983.

———. *Service Evangelism.* Philadelphia: Westminster, 1983.

Kantonen, T. A. *Theology of Evangelism.* Philadelphia: Muhlenberg, 1954.

Leavall, Roland Q. *Evangelism: Christ's Imperative Commission.* Revised edition. Nashville: Broadman, 1979.

Marsh, Clinton M. *Evangelism Is . . .* Louisville: Westminster/John Knox, 1998.

McGavran, Donald A. *Effective Evangelism: A Theological Mandate.* Phillipsburg: Presbyterian and Reformed, 1988.

McIntosh, Duncan. *The Everyday Evangelist.* Valley Forge, Pa.: Judson, 1984.

Miles, Delos. *Church Growth: A Mighty River.* Nashville: Broadman, 1981.

———. *Introduction to Evangelism.* Nashville: Broadman, 1983.

———. *Master Principles of Evangelism.* Nashville: Broadman, 1982.

———. *Overcoming Barriers to Witnessing.* Nashville: Broadman, 1984.

Read, David H. C. *Go Make Disciples.* Nashville: Abingdon, 1978.

Rudin, A. James, and Marvin R. Wilson, editors. *A Time to Speak: The Evangelical-Jewish Encounter.* Grand Rapids: Eerdmans, 1987.

Schaller, Lyle E. *Activating the Passive Church: Diagnosis and Treatment.* Nashville: Abingdon, 1981.

Slaughter, Michael. *Real Followers.* Nashville: Abingdon, 1999.

Smith, Donald P. *Congregations Alive.* Philadelphia: Westminster, 1981.

Southard, Samuel. *Pastoral Evangelism.* Nashville: Broadman, 1962.

Sweazey, George E. *The Church as Evangelist.* New York: Harper & Row, 1978.

———. *Effective Evangelism.* Revised edition. New York: Harper & Row, 1976.

Trueblood, Elton. *The Company of the Committed.* New York: Harper & Row, 1961.

———. *The Incendiary Fellowship.* New York: Harper & Row, 1967.

Wagner, Peter C. *Your Church Can Grow.* Ventura, Calif.: Regal, 1976.

Walker, Alan. *The New Evangelism.* Nashville: Abingdon, 1975.

Wallis, Jim. *The Call to Conversion.* San Francisco: Harper & Row, 1983.

Watson, David. *I Believe in Evangelism.* Grand Rapids: Eerdmans, 1976.

Wells, David F. *God the Evangelist.* Grand Rapids: Eerdmans, 1987.

Willimon, William H. *The Gospel for the Person Who Has Everything* (Valley Forge, Pa.: Judson, 1978).

Wirt, Sherwood Eliot, editor. *Evangelism: The Next Ten Years.* Waco, Tex.: Word, 1978.